CREATIVE MANDALA COLORING: 51 STRESS-RELIEVING ADULT COLORING BOOK PATTERNS FEATURING SYMMETRICAL & RELAXING MANDALAS

Volume 1

By: Marie's Coloring

Print Edition 2015

Sign up to receive FREE weekly print-and-color patterns delivered straight to your inbox! Just type this URL into your browser: https://mirdock.leadpages.co/mariescoloring

INTRODUCTION

The word *mandala* is loosely translated to mean "circle" in the Indian language of Sanskrit. Used by Hindus and Buddhists for centuries, these ancient circles of geometrical symmetry represent wholeness, and are a reminder of our relationship to the universe and infinite spiritual powers.

The symbols have been used in meditative practice to help an individual discover inner meaning, reduce stress and to learn more about their spiritual journey or path, among other benefits. Meditation on mandalas also allows an individual to focus on the creative aspect of the design while allowing the mind to slow down.

Now you too can benefit from the calming influence of the mandala. By coloring each design you go into the art and become one with it. Coloring is a relaxing way to still the mind and develop your creative side. These designs are meant to soothe and relieve tension.

Coloring pencils work well for these designs, as do fine tip markers. Allow your imagination to explore different color combinations as you explore your spiritual, creative side and have fun!

Meanings of different colors:

Purple: Spiritual
Blue: Emotional healing, meditation, inner peace
Red: Passion, strength, high energy
Gold: Success, triumph, achievement
Orange: Intuition, self-awareness, creativity
Green: Psychic ability, physical healing, love of nature
White: Spiritual focus
Black: Deep thinking, individuality, mystery
Silver: Feminine energy, sensitive, emotional

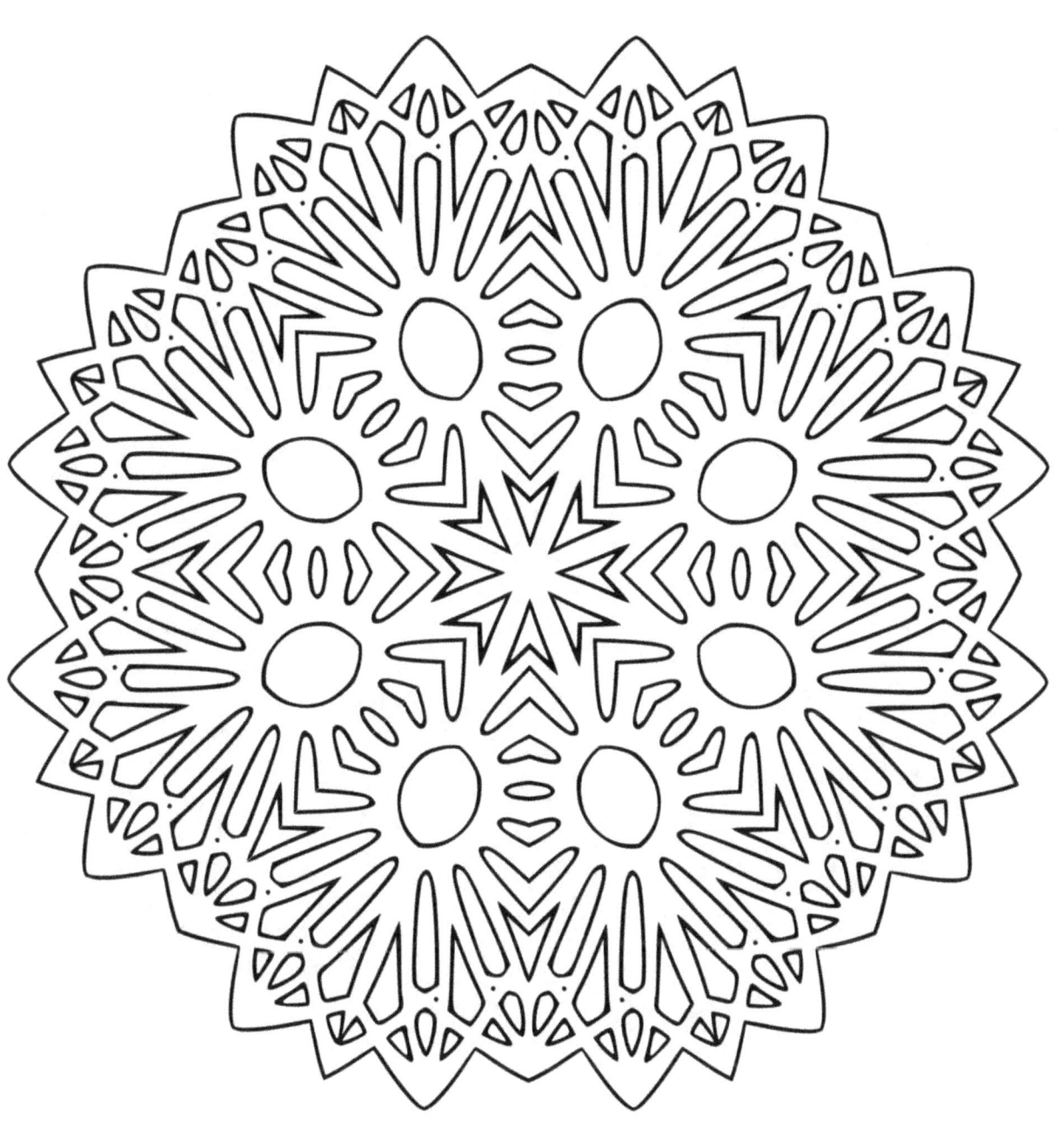

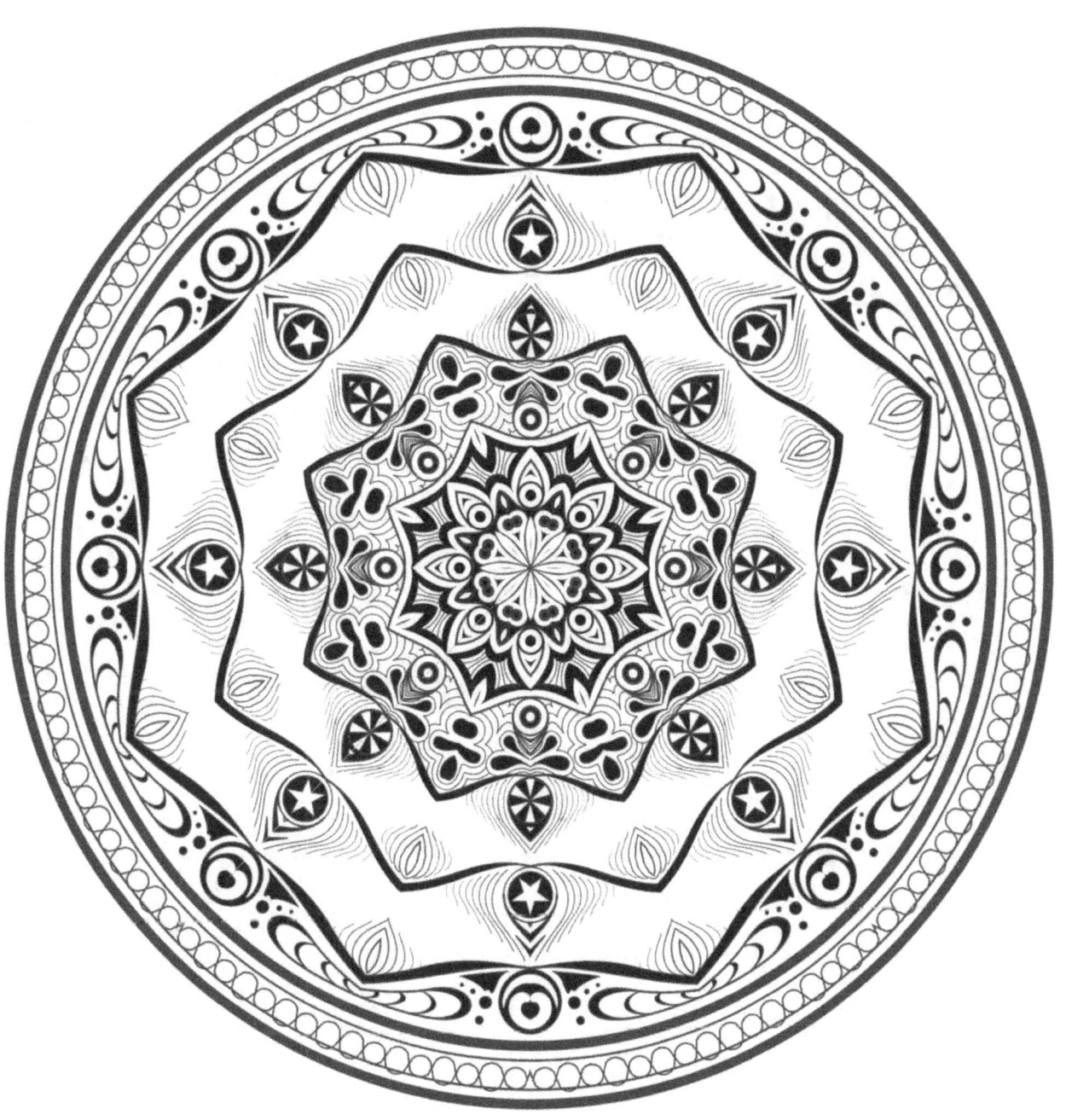

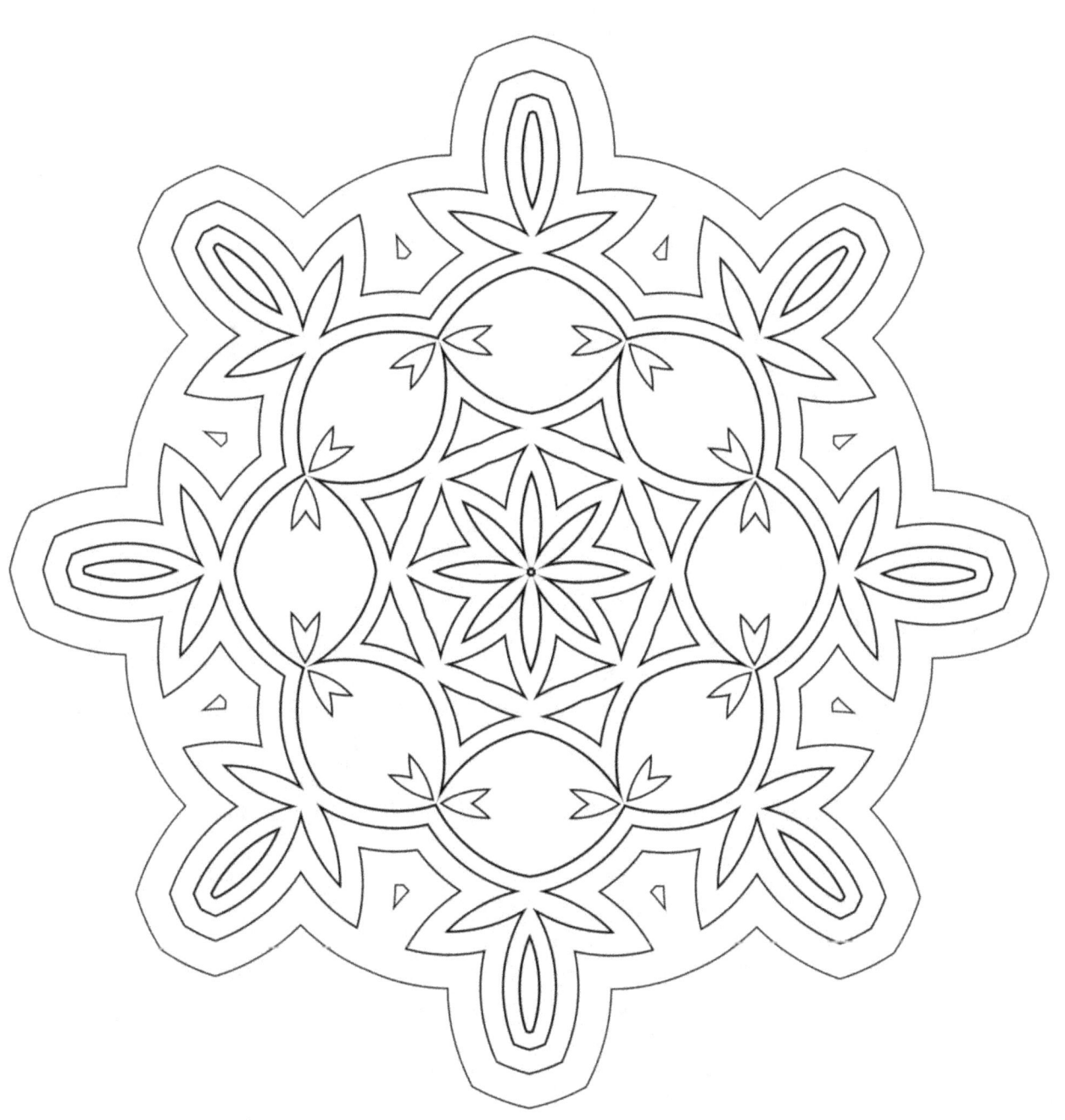

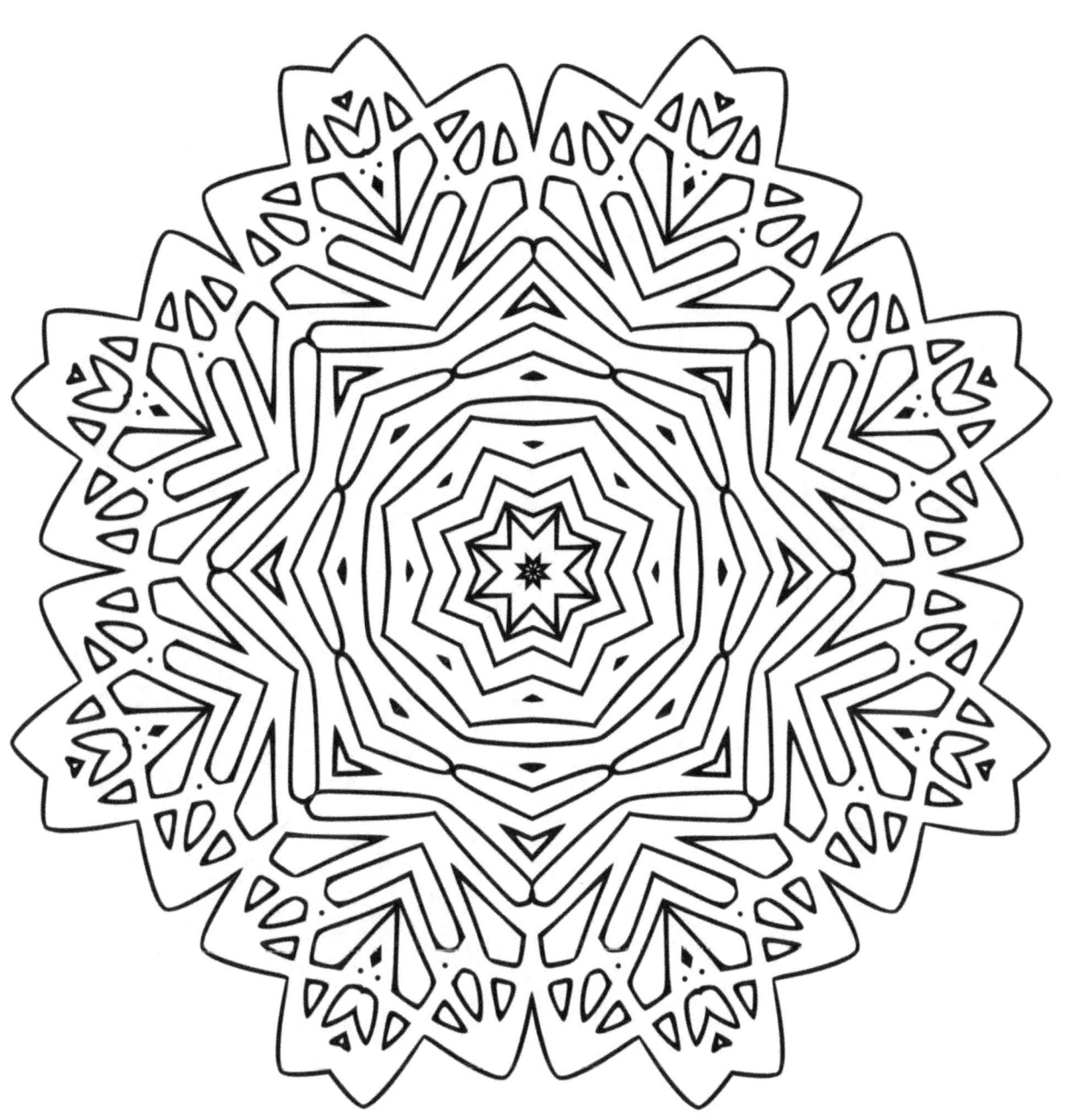

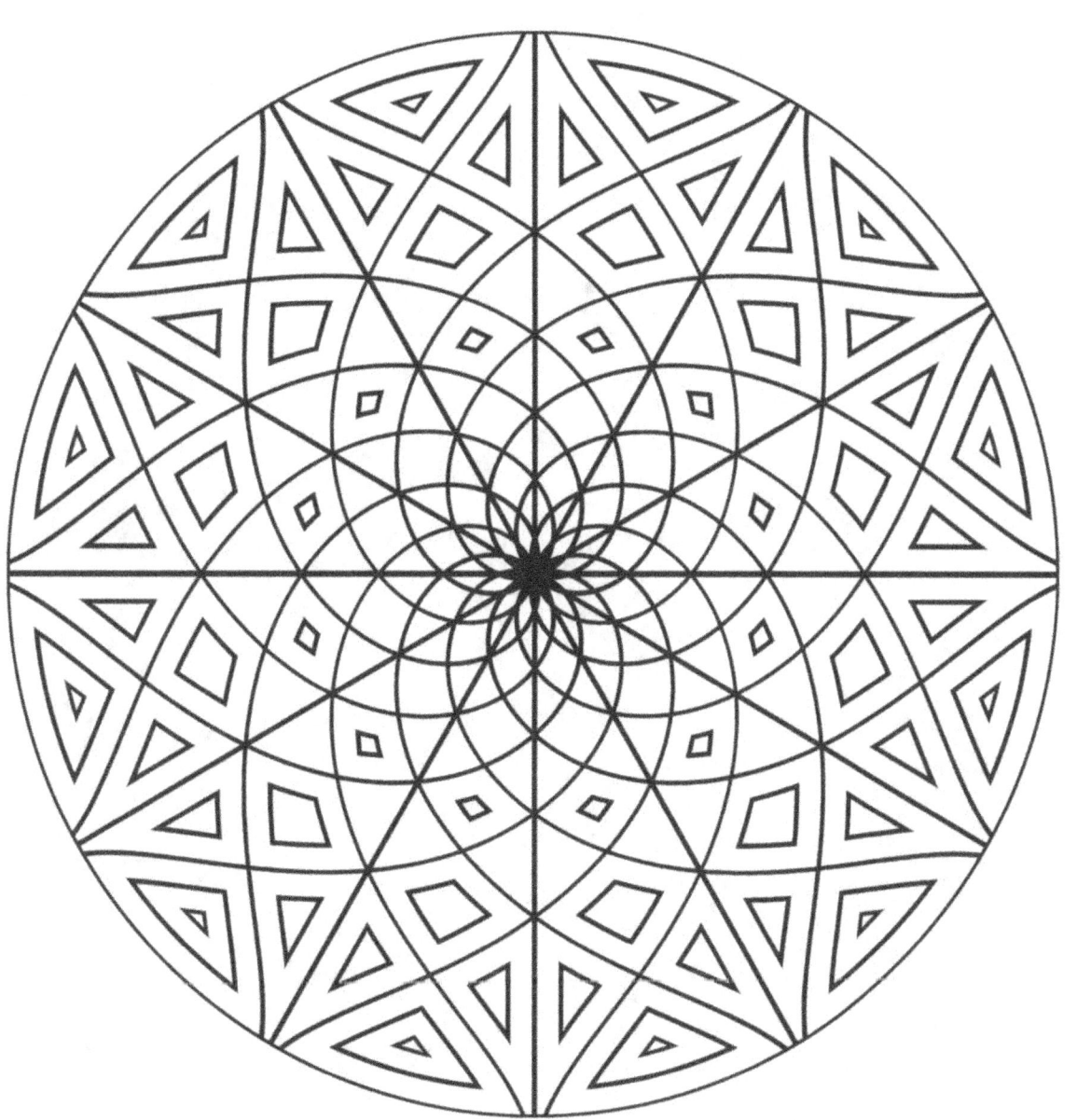

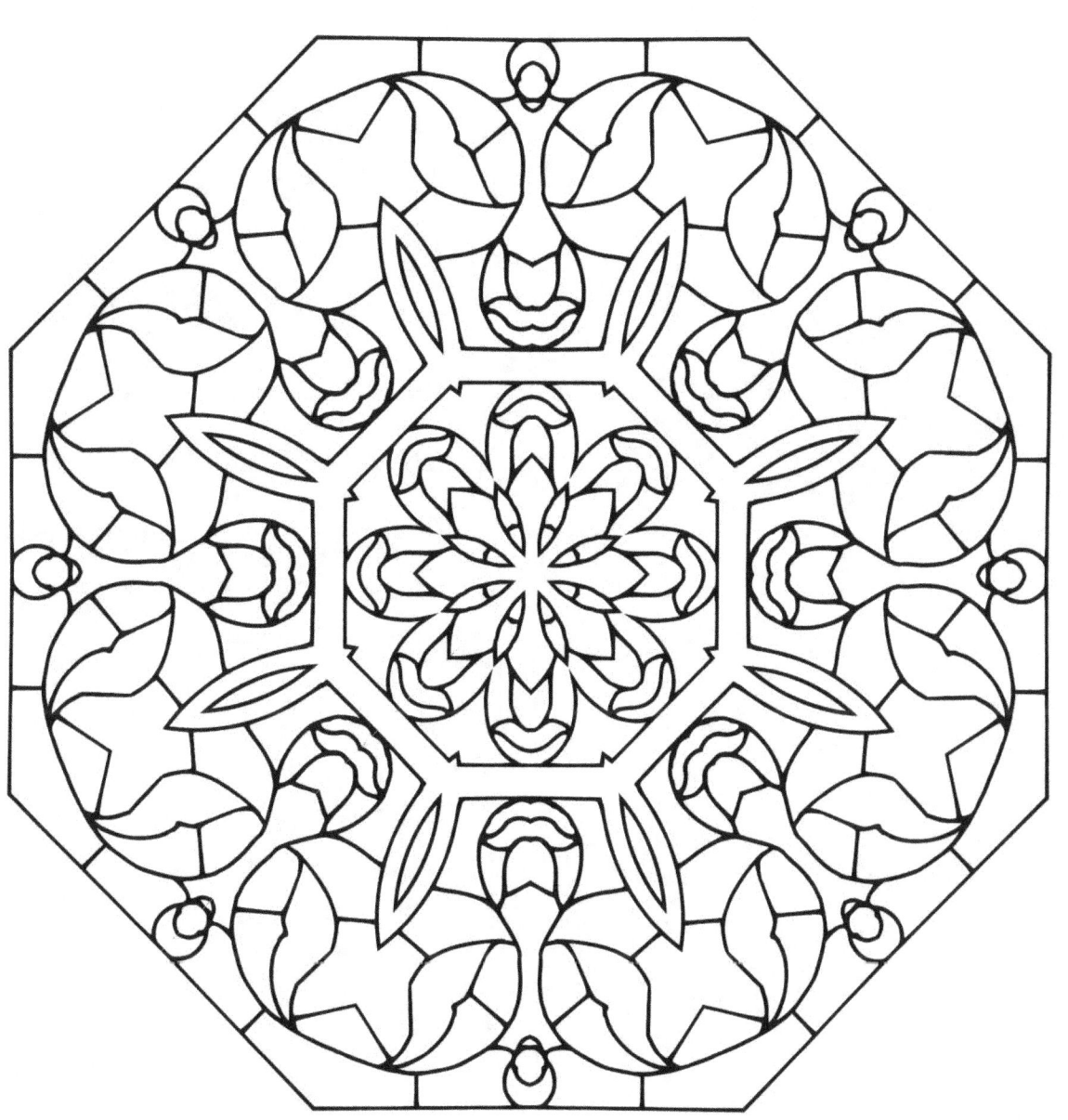

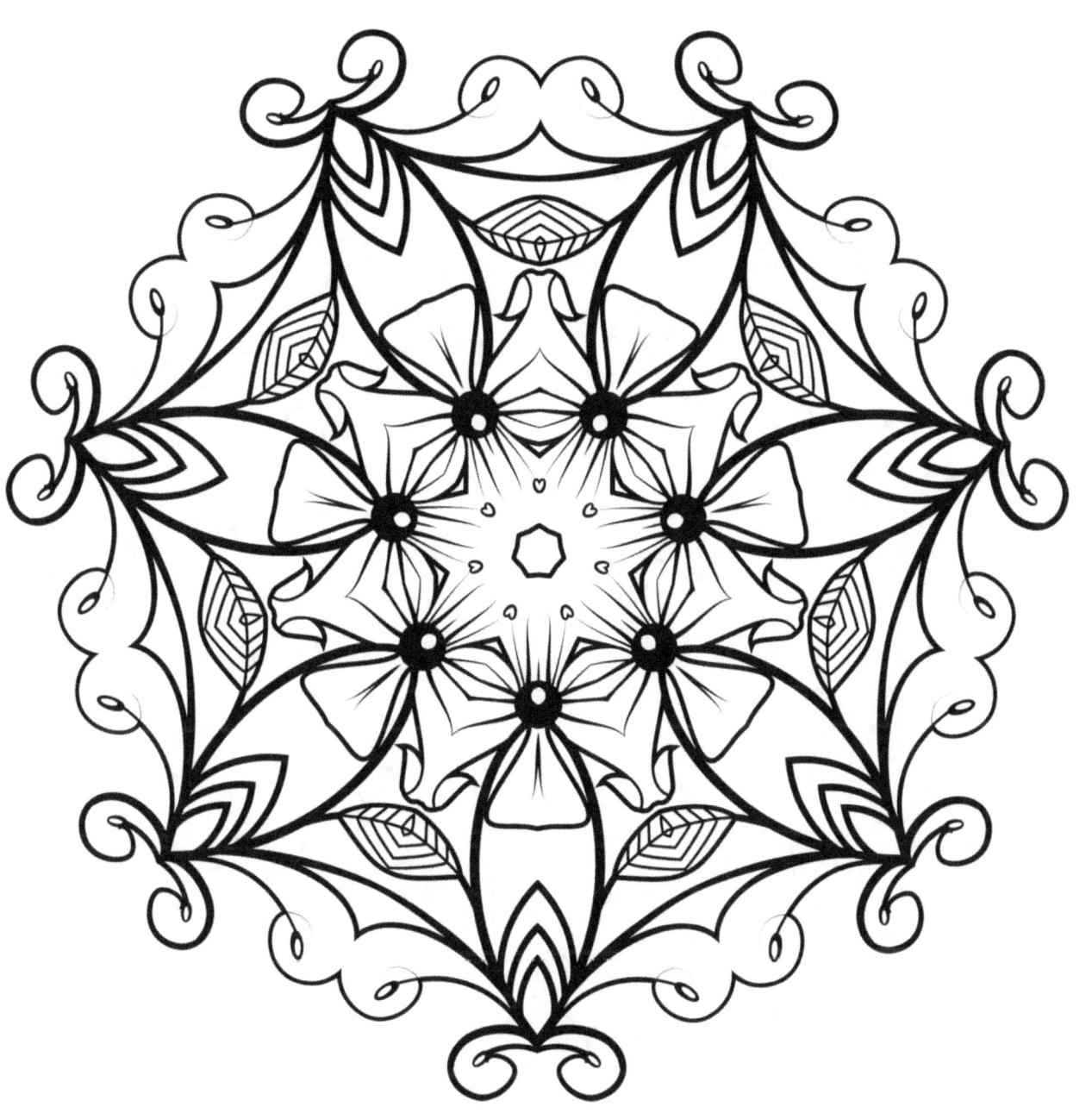

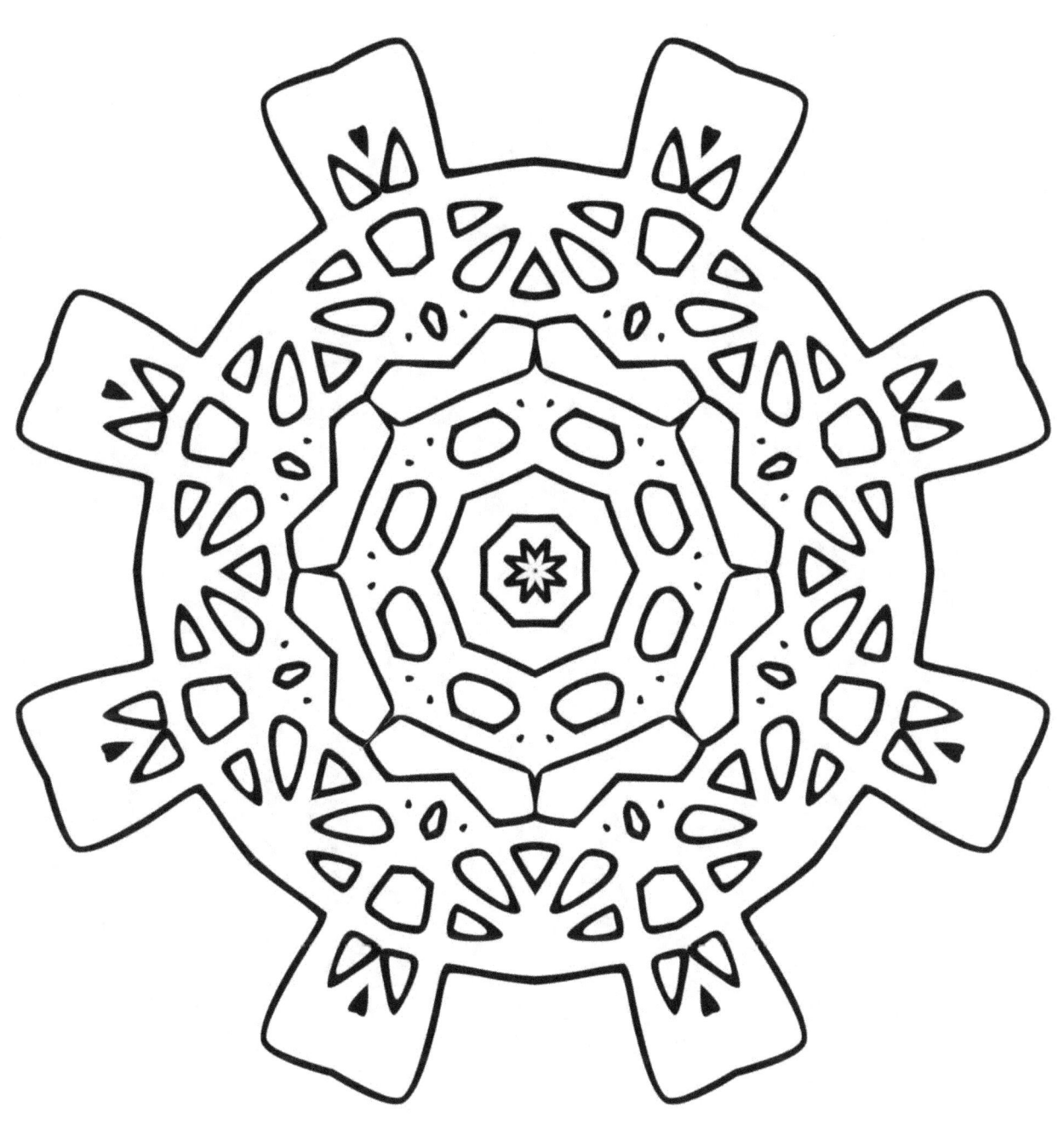

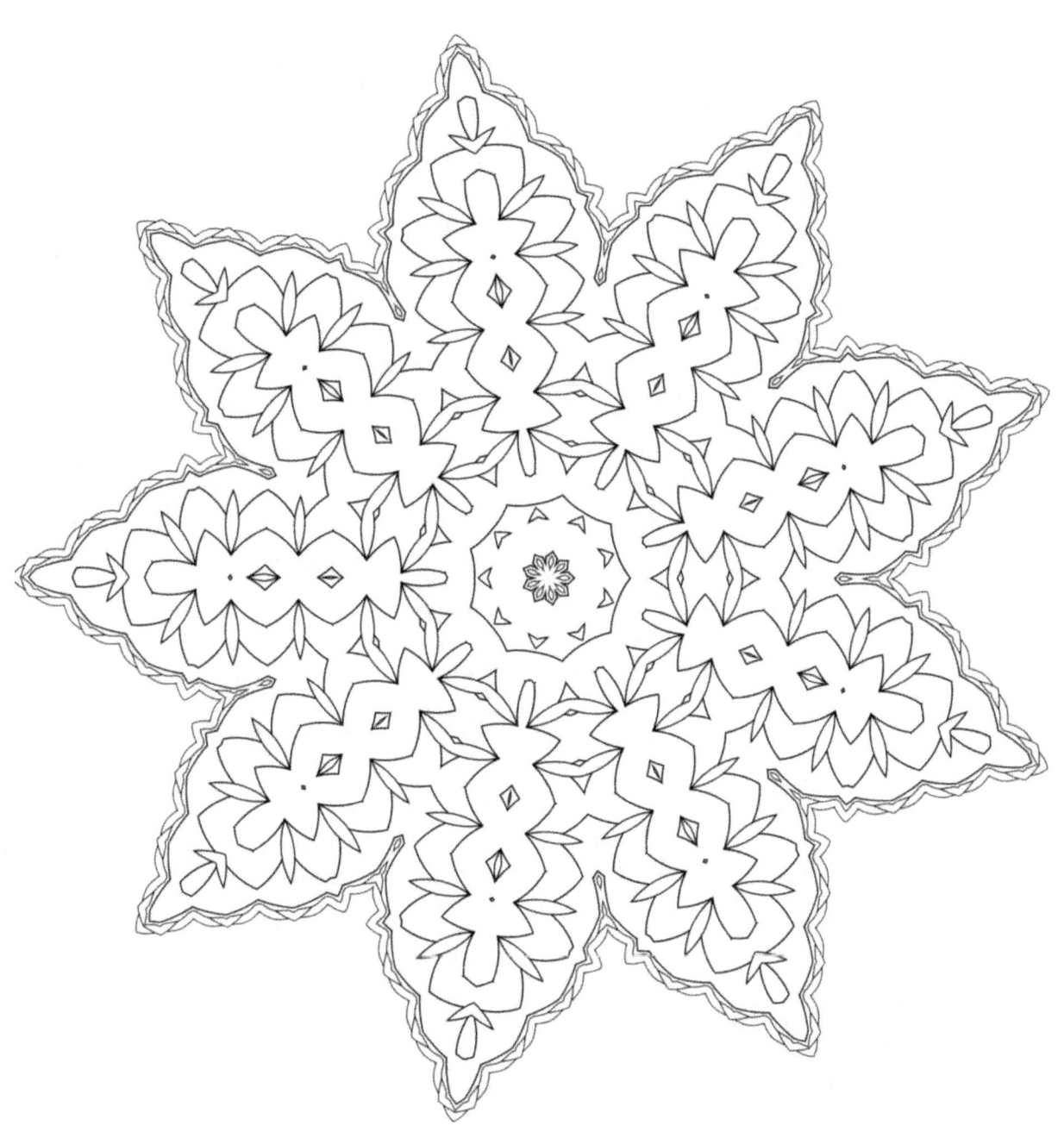

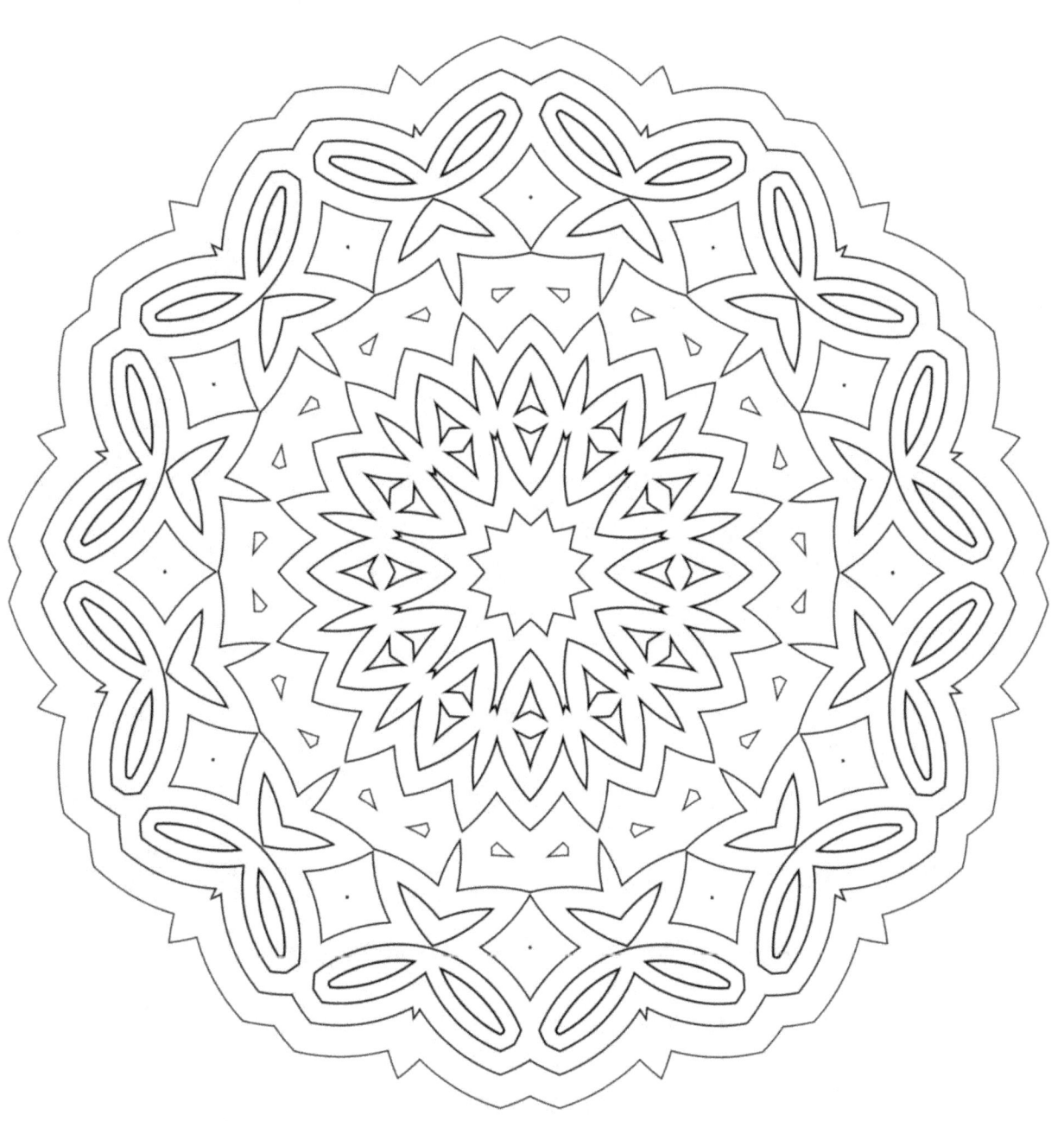

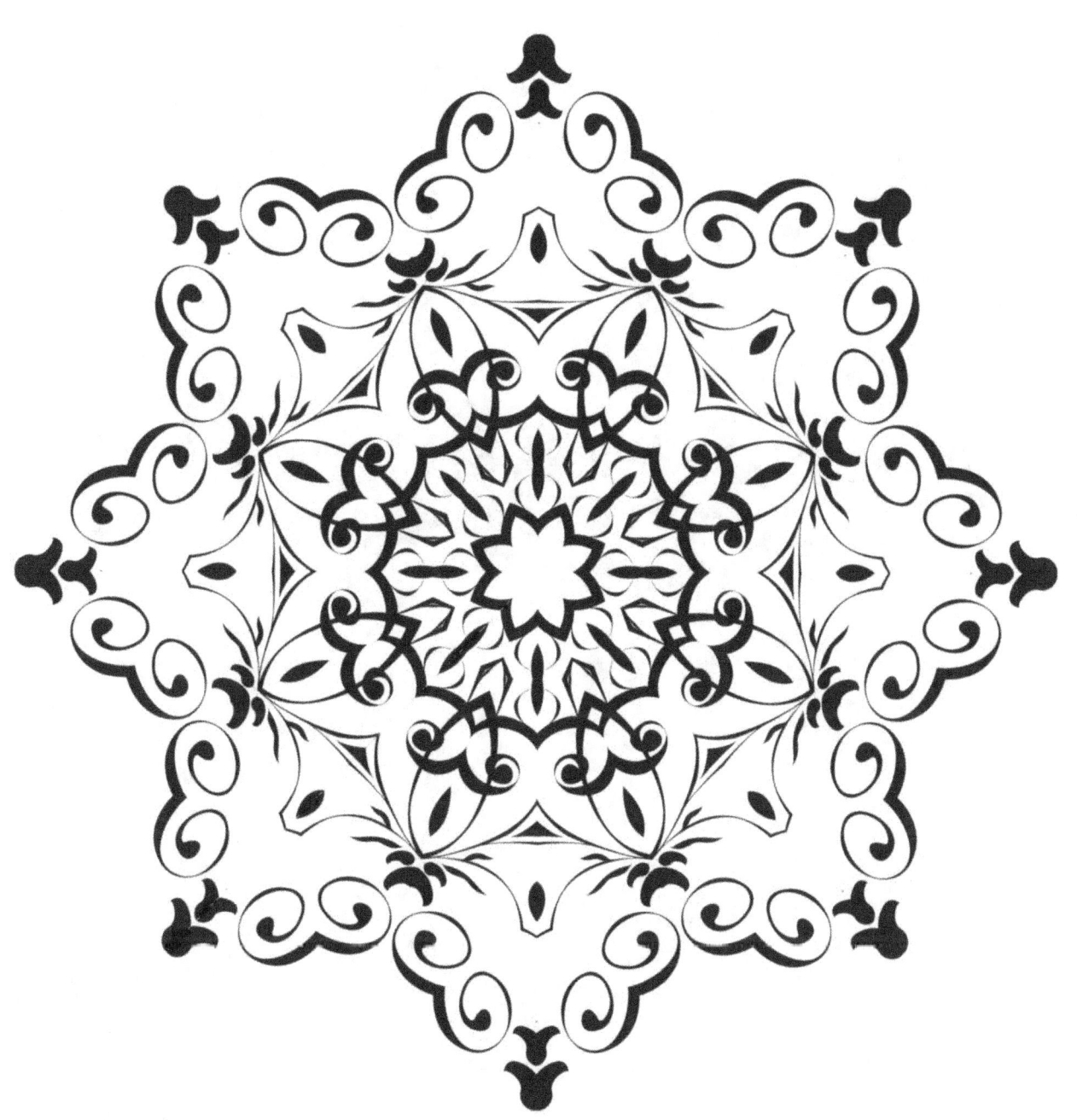

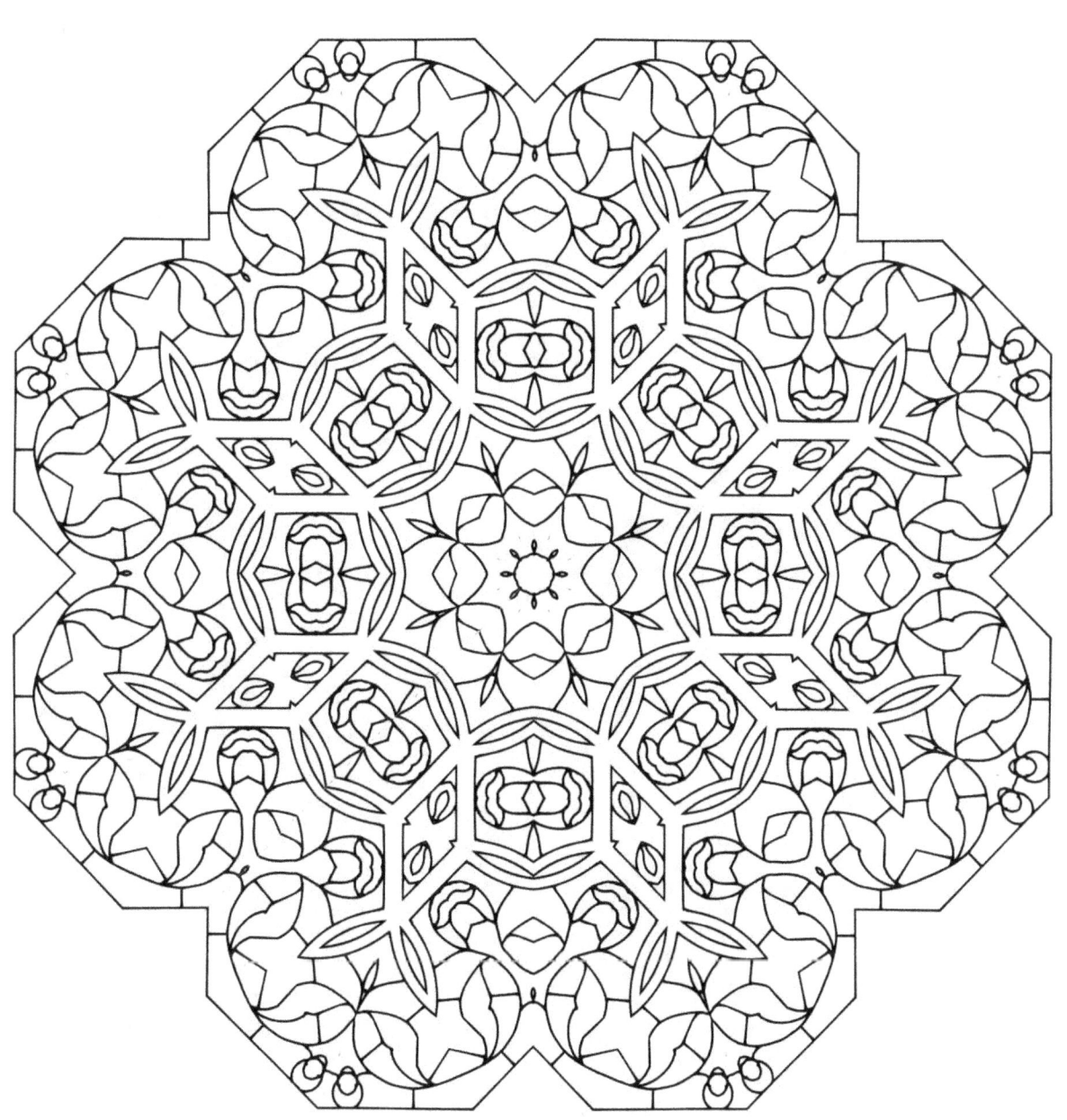

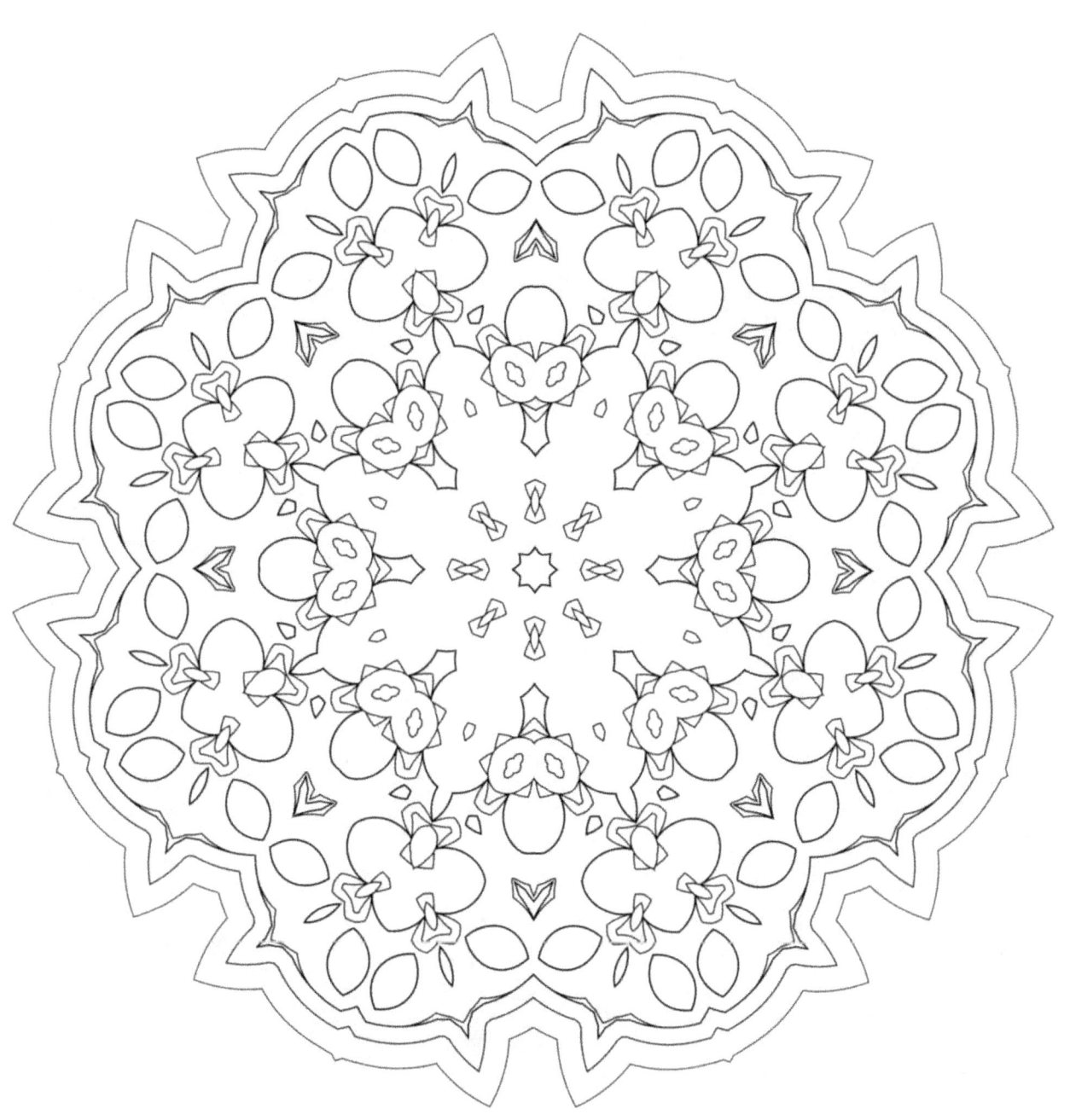

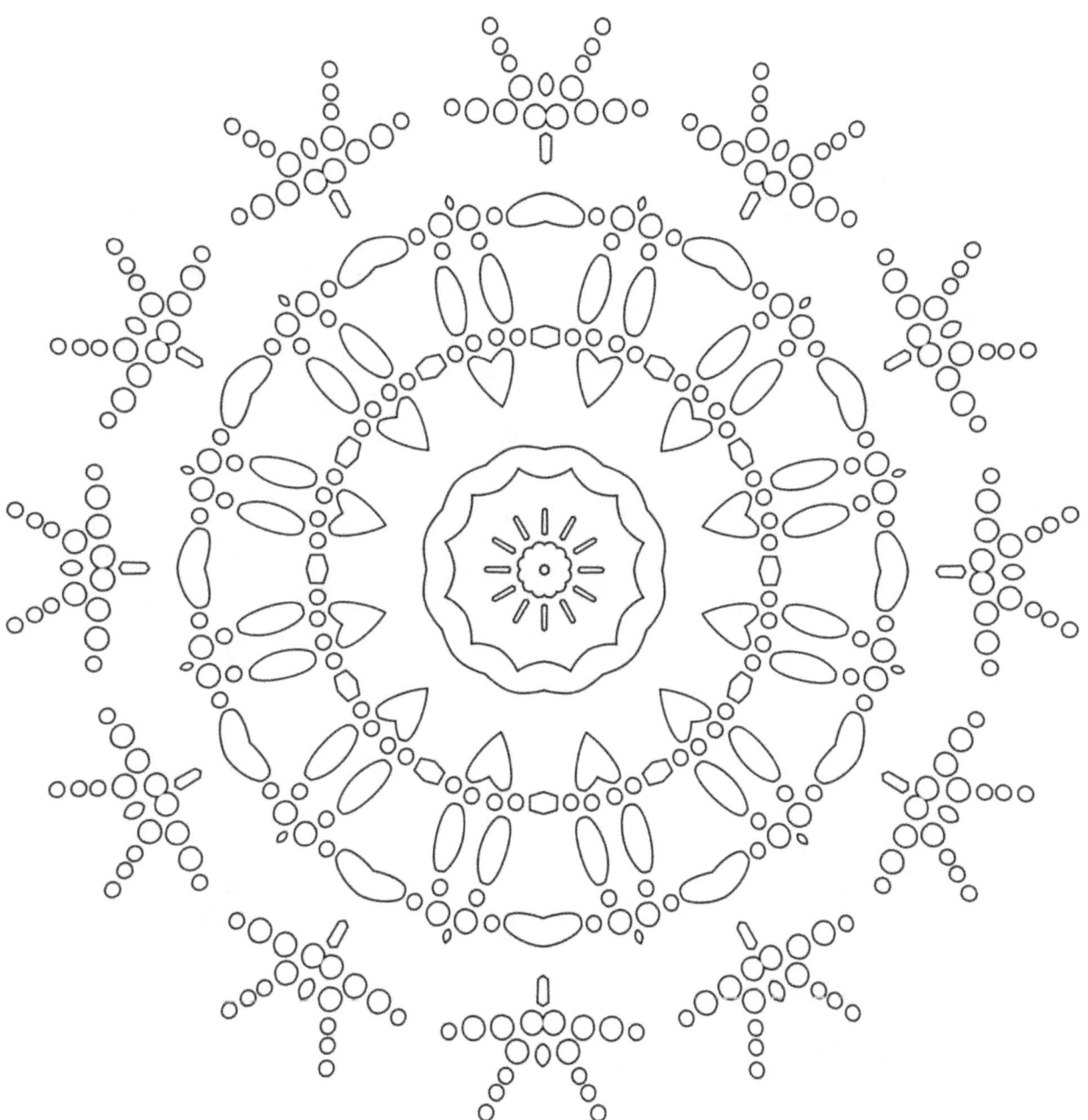

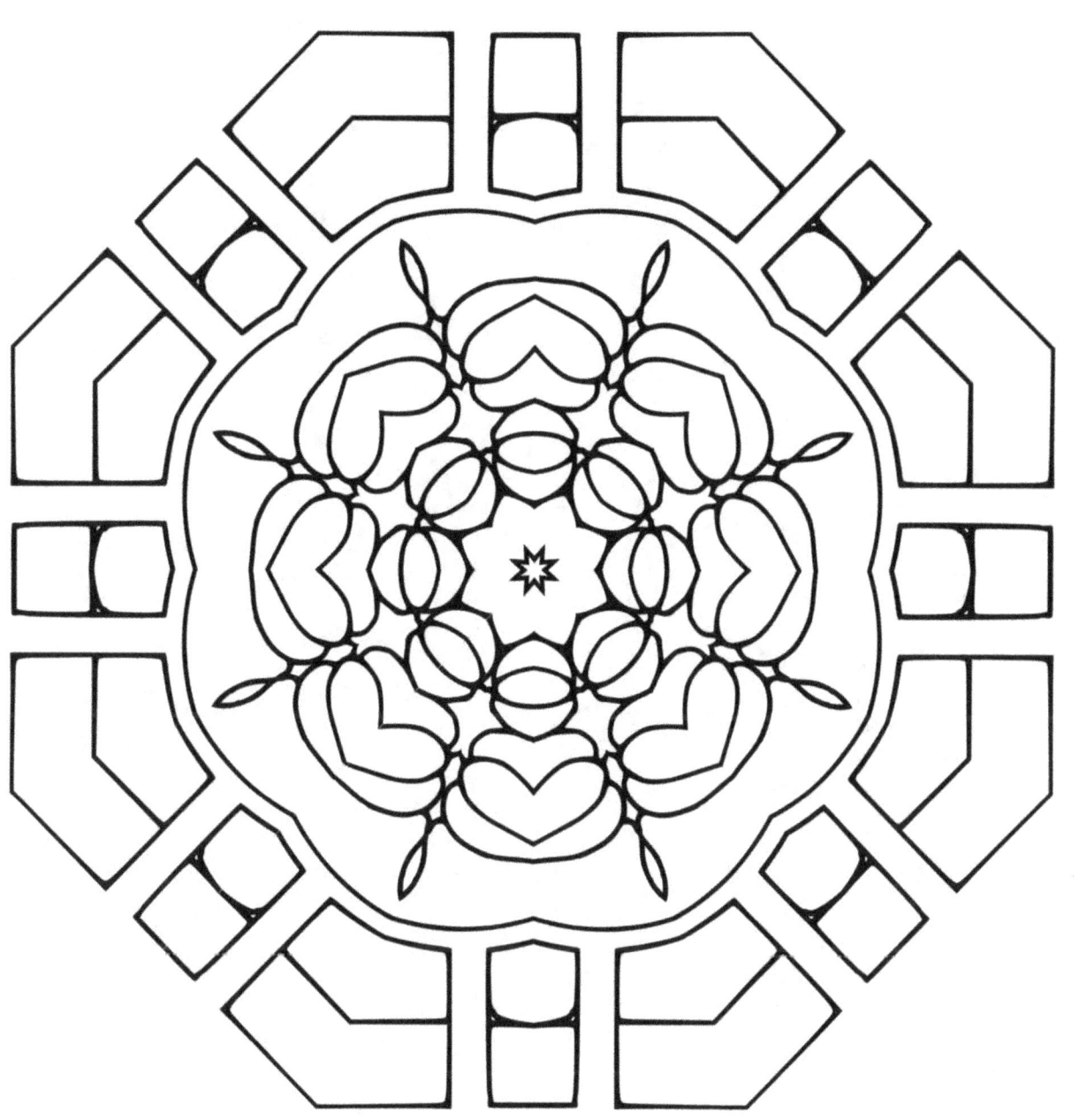

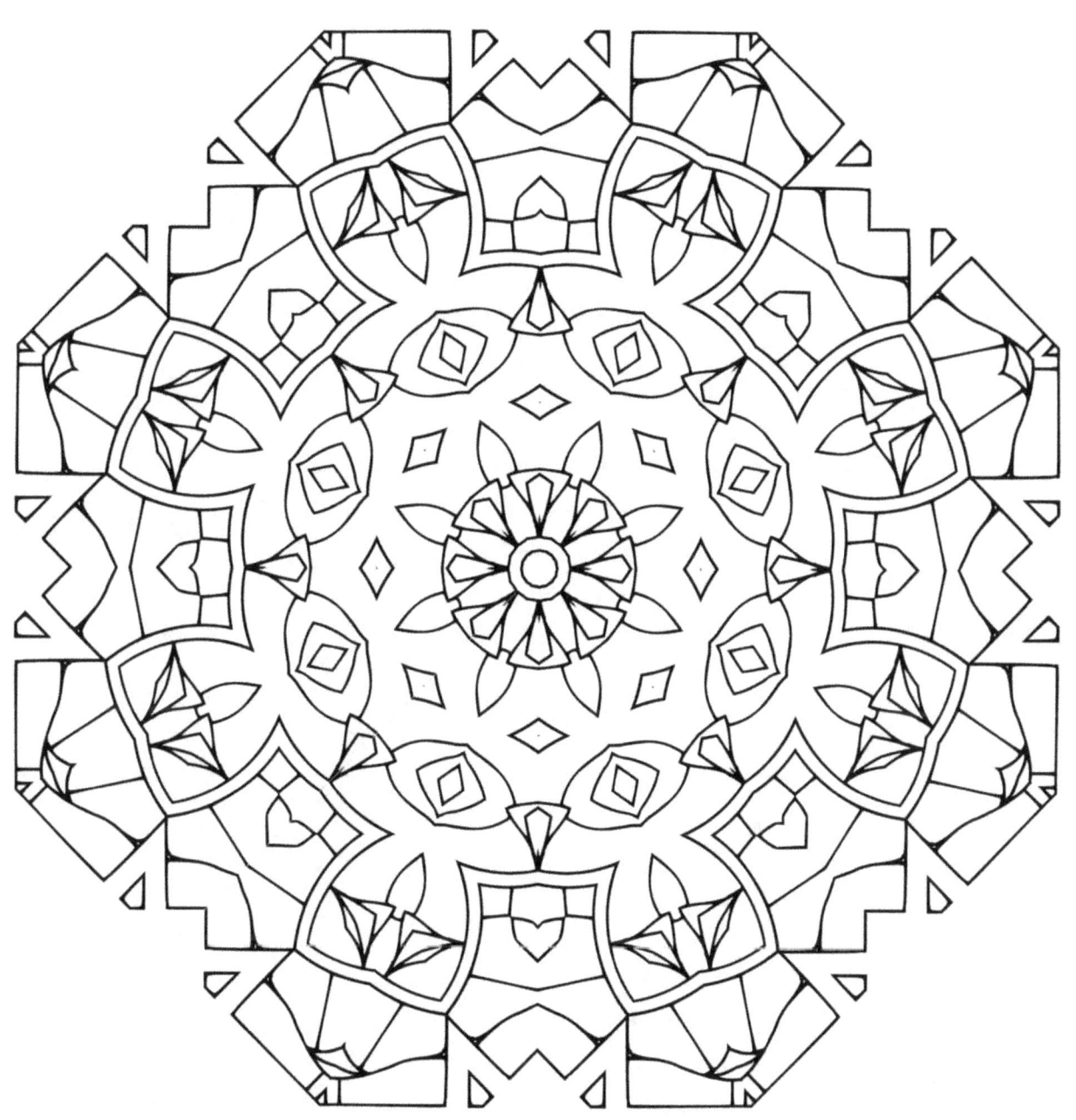

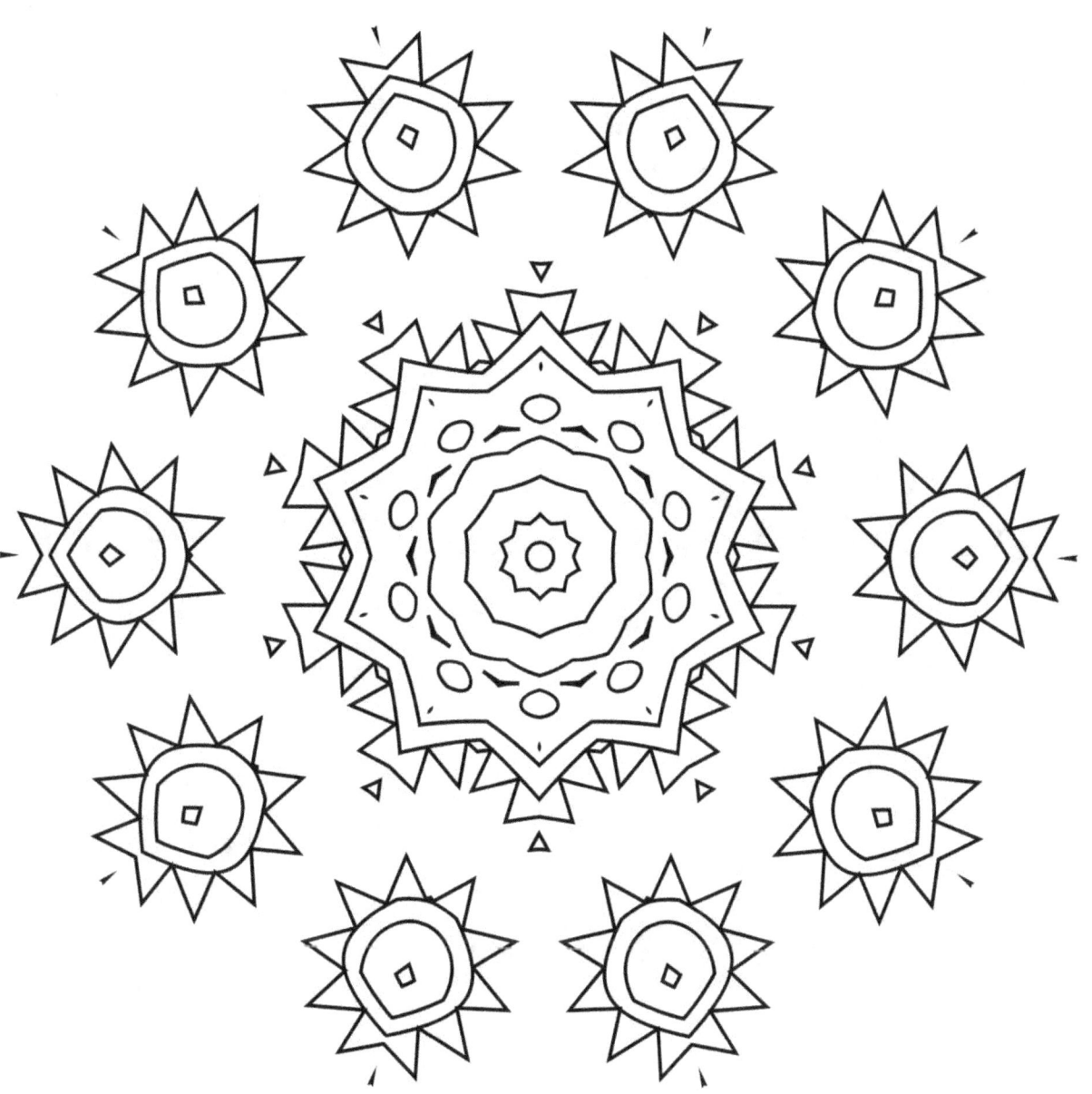

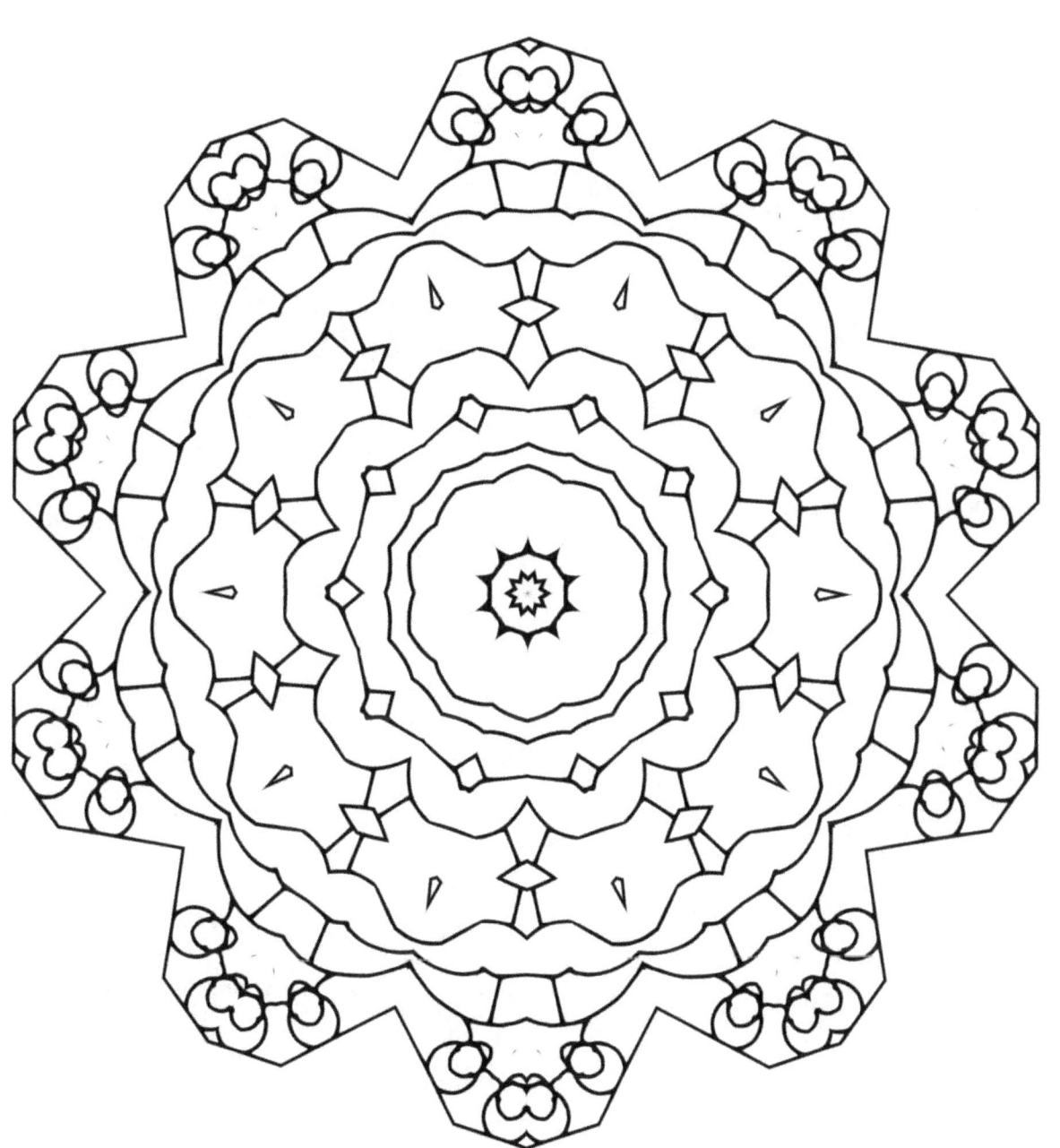

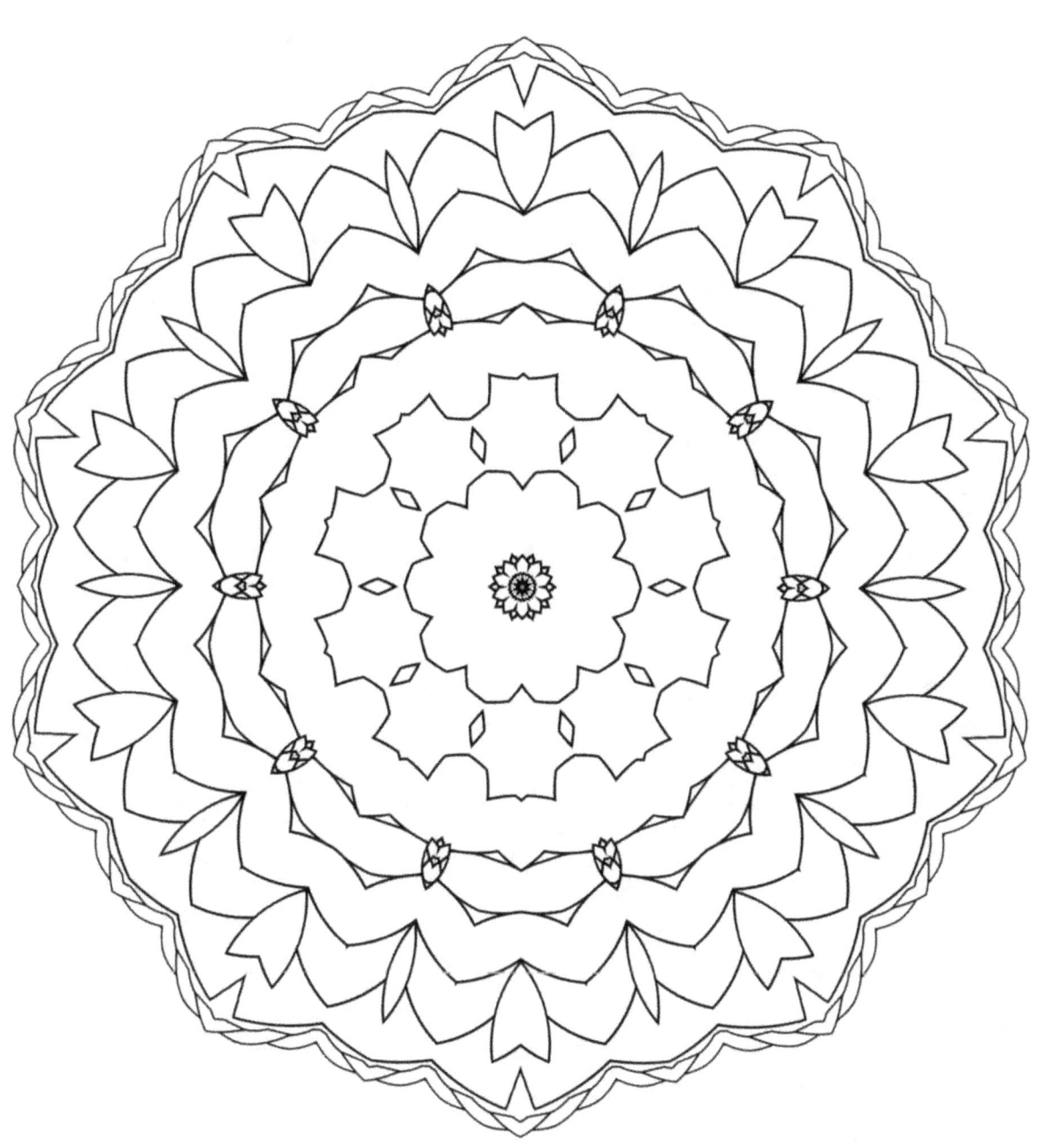

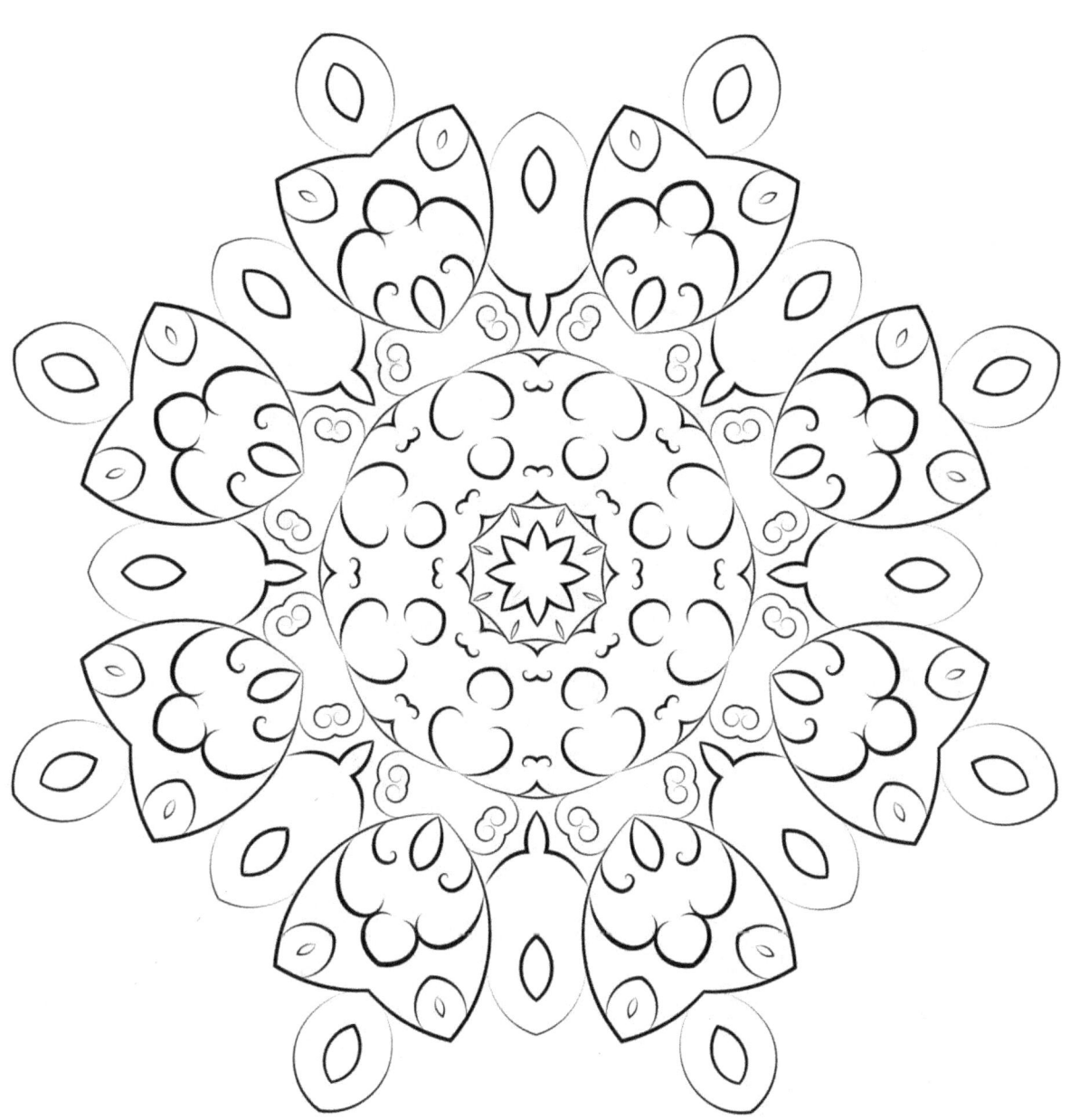

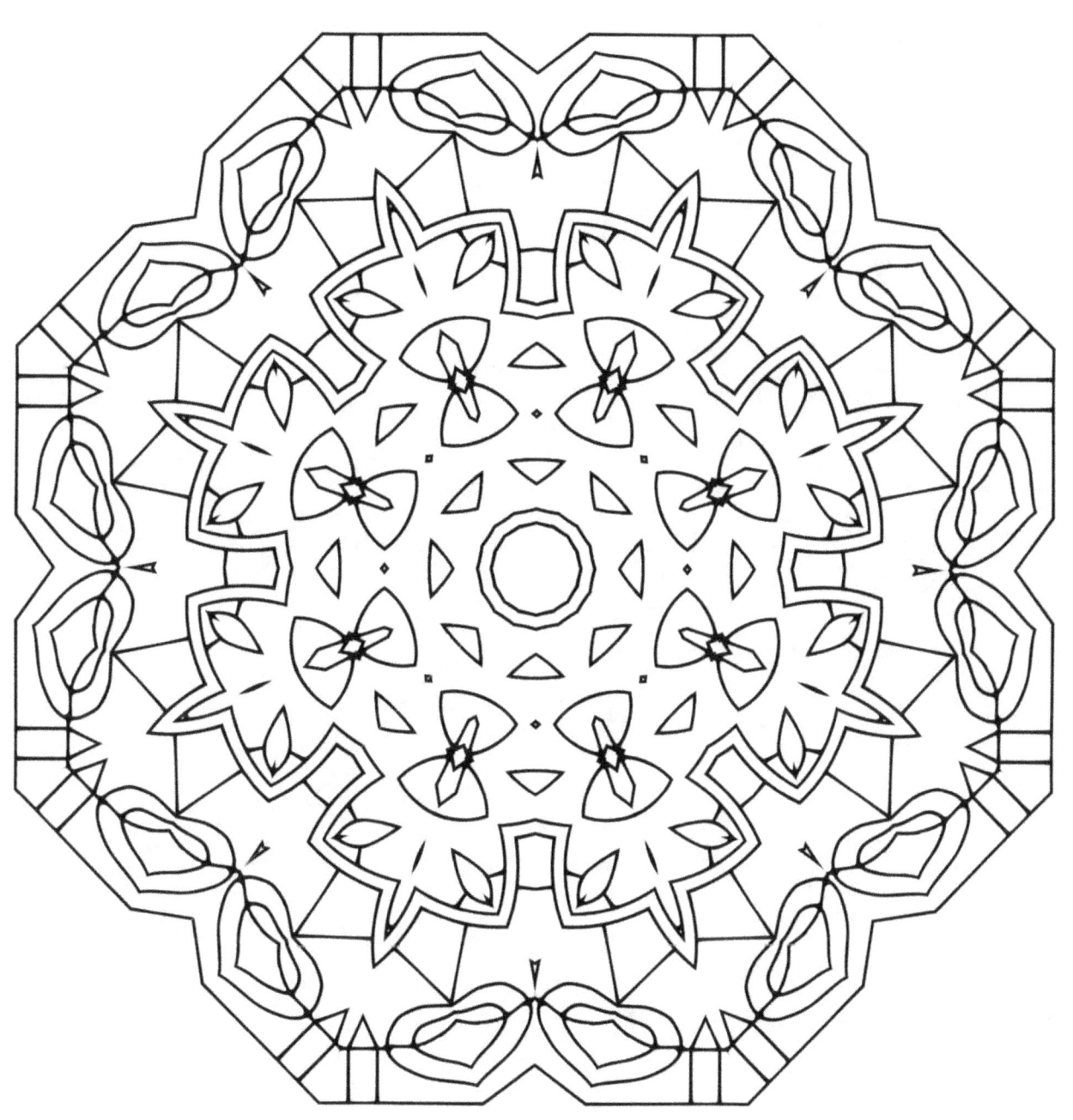

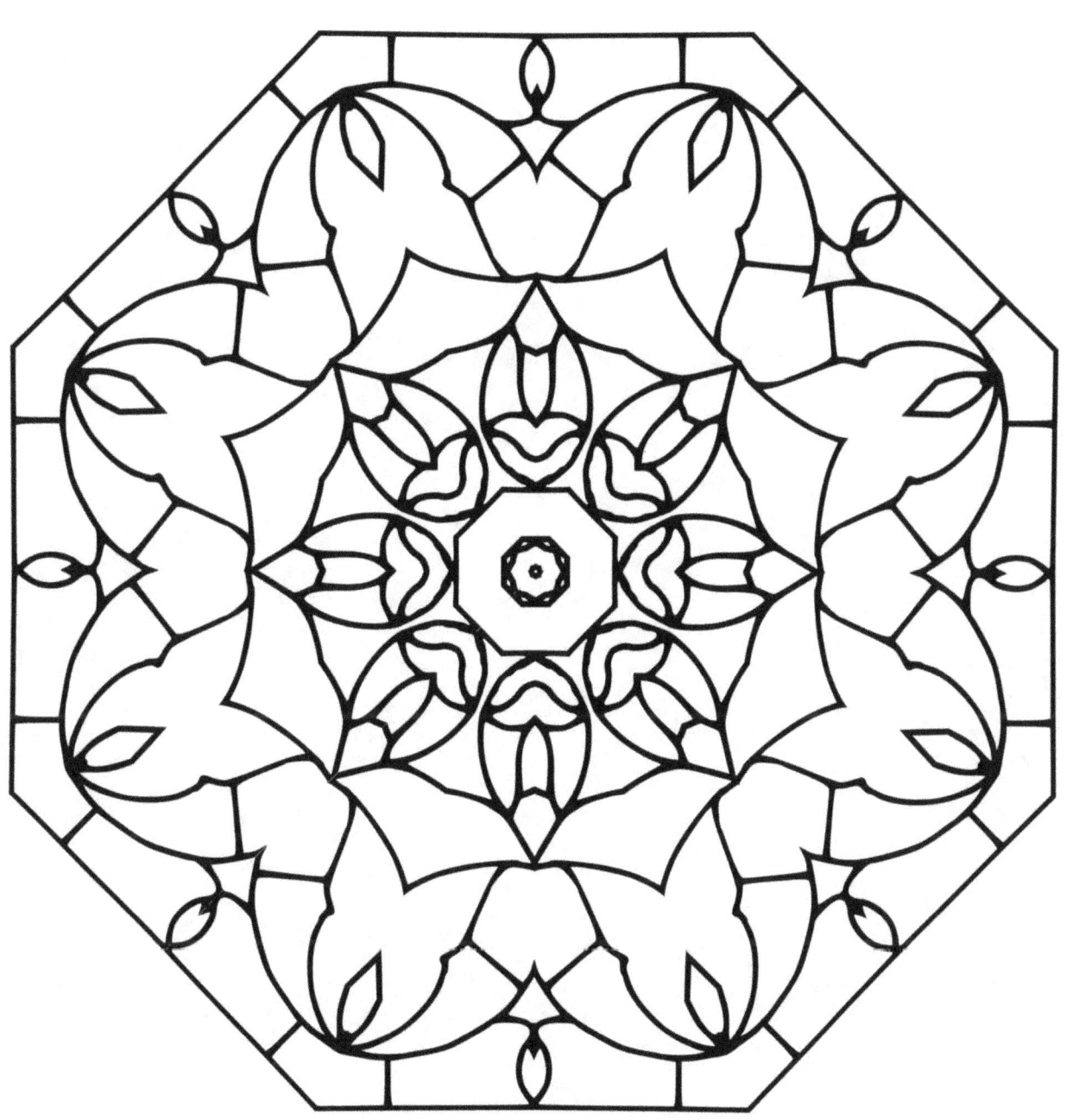

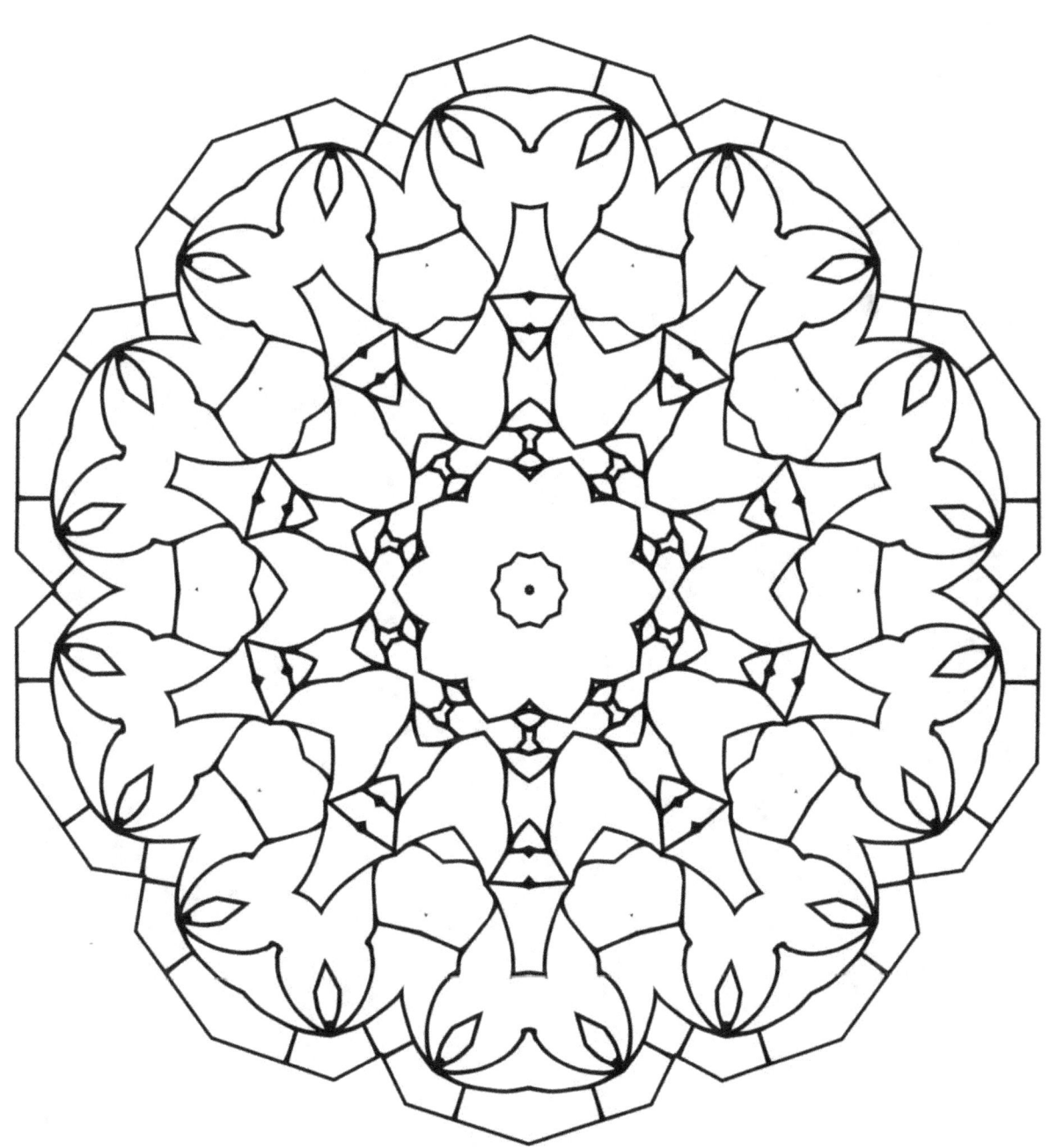

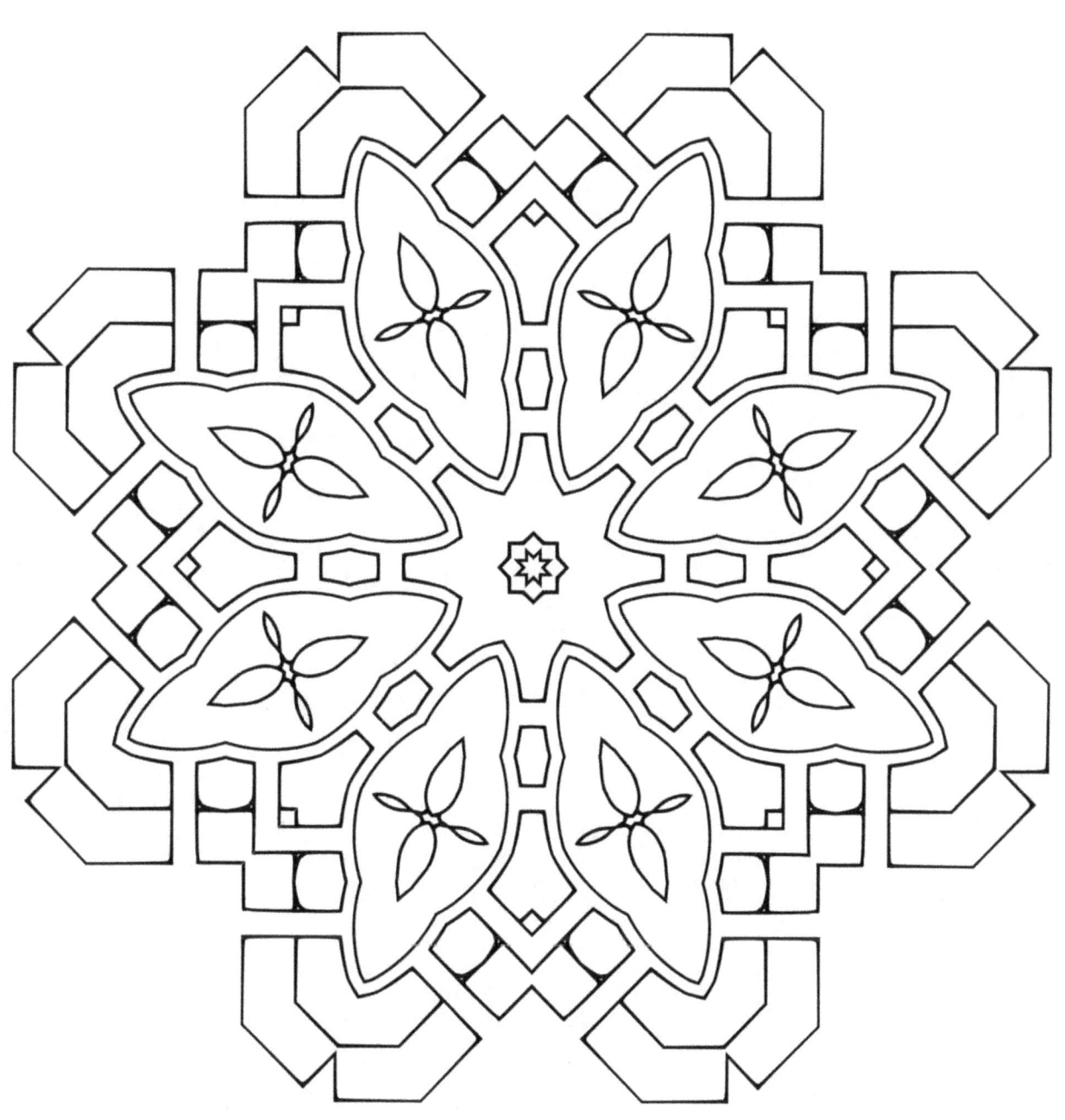

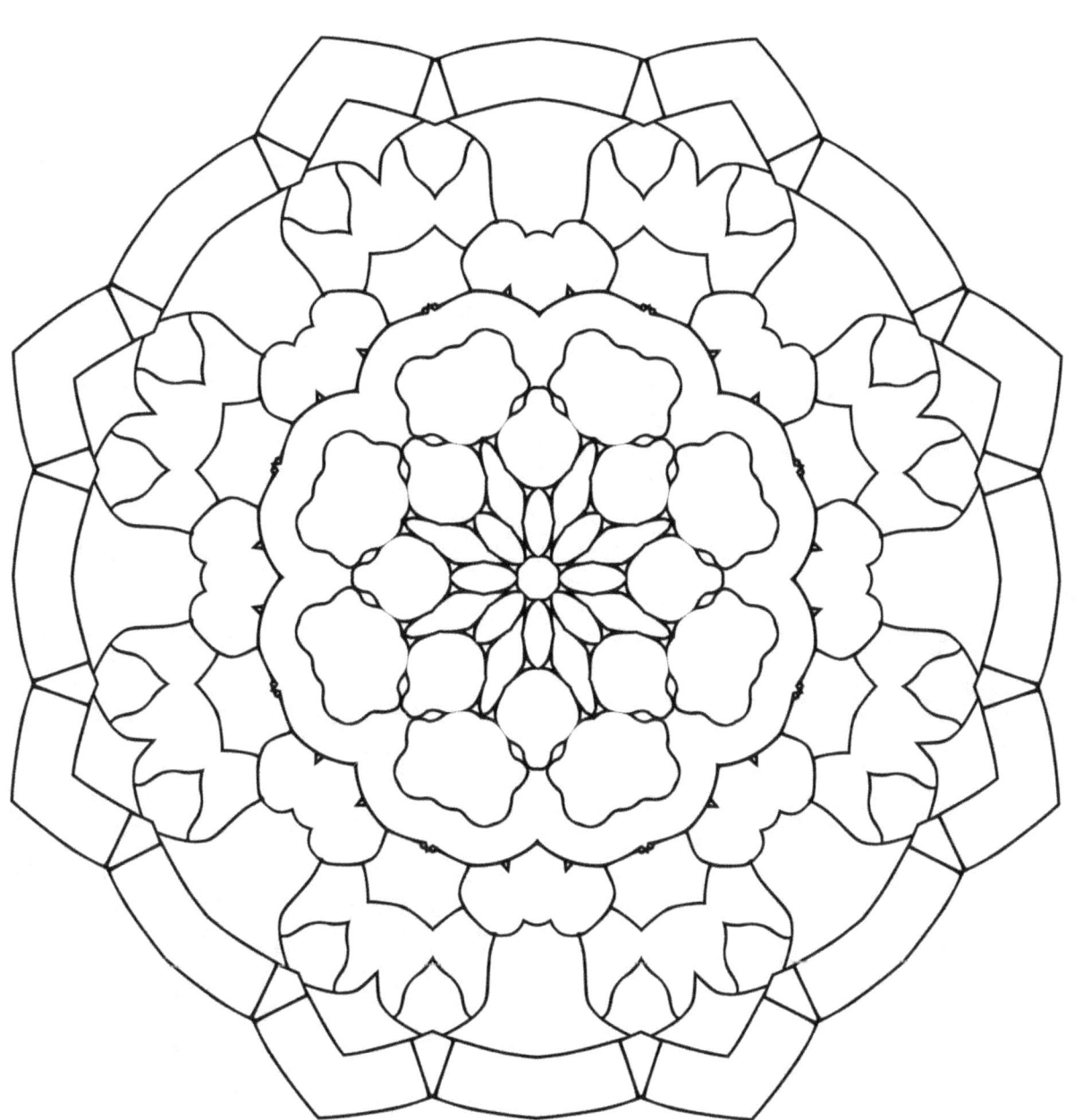

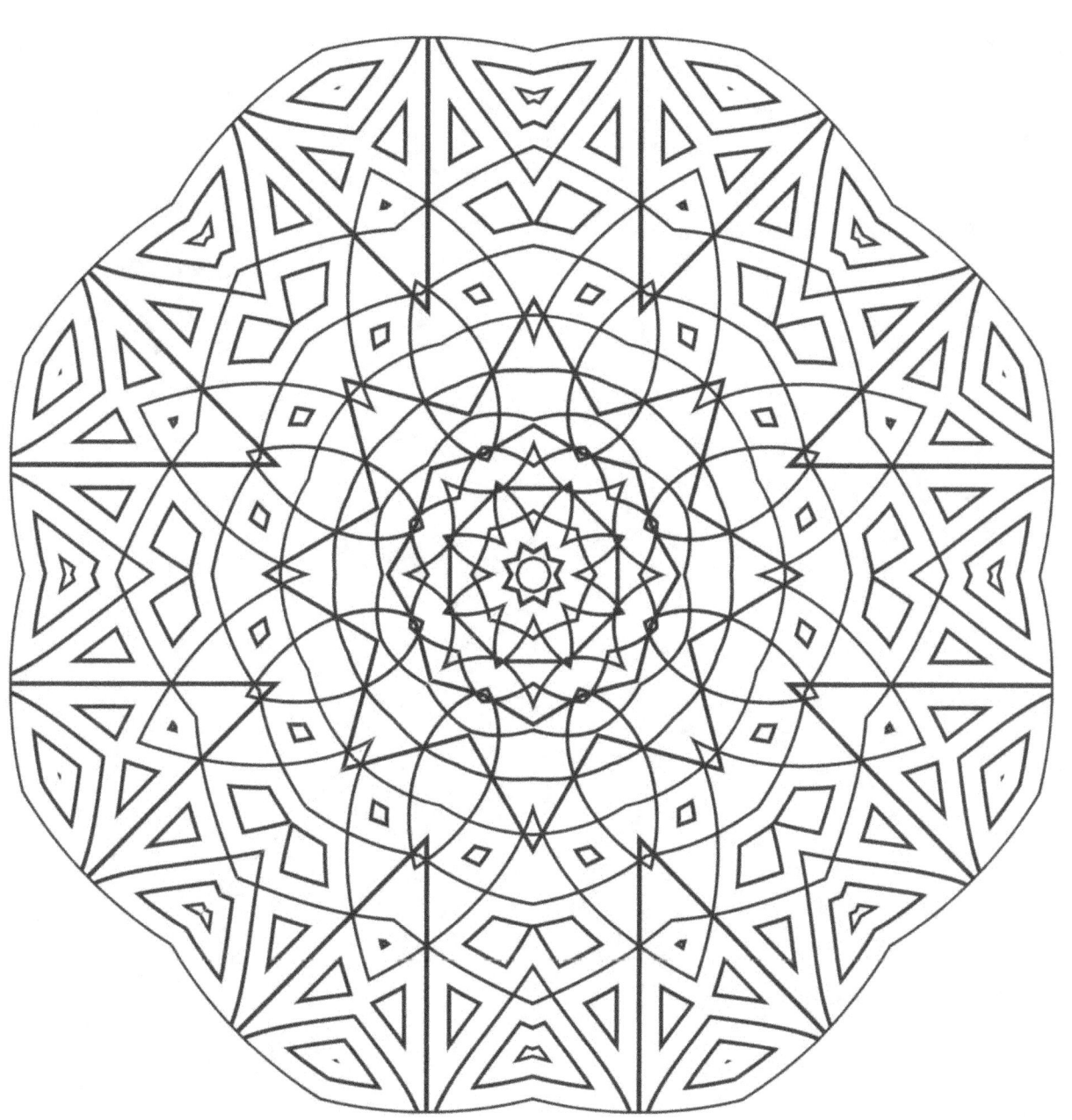

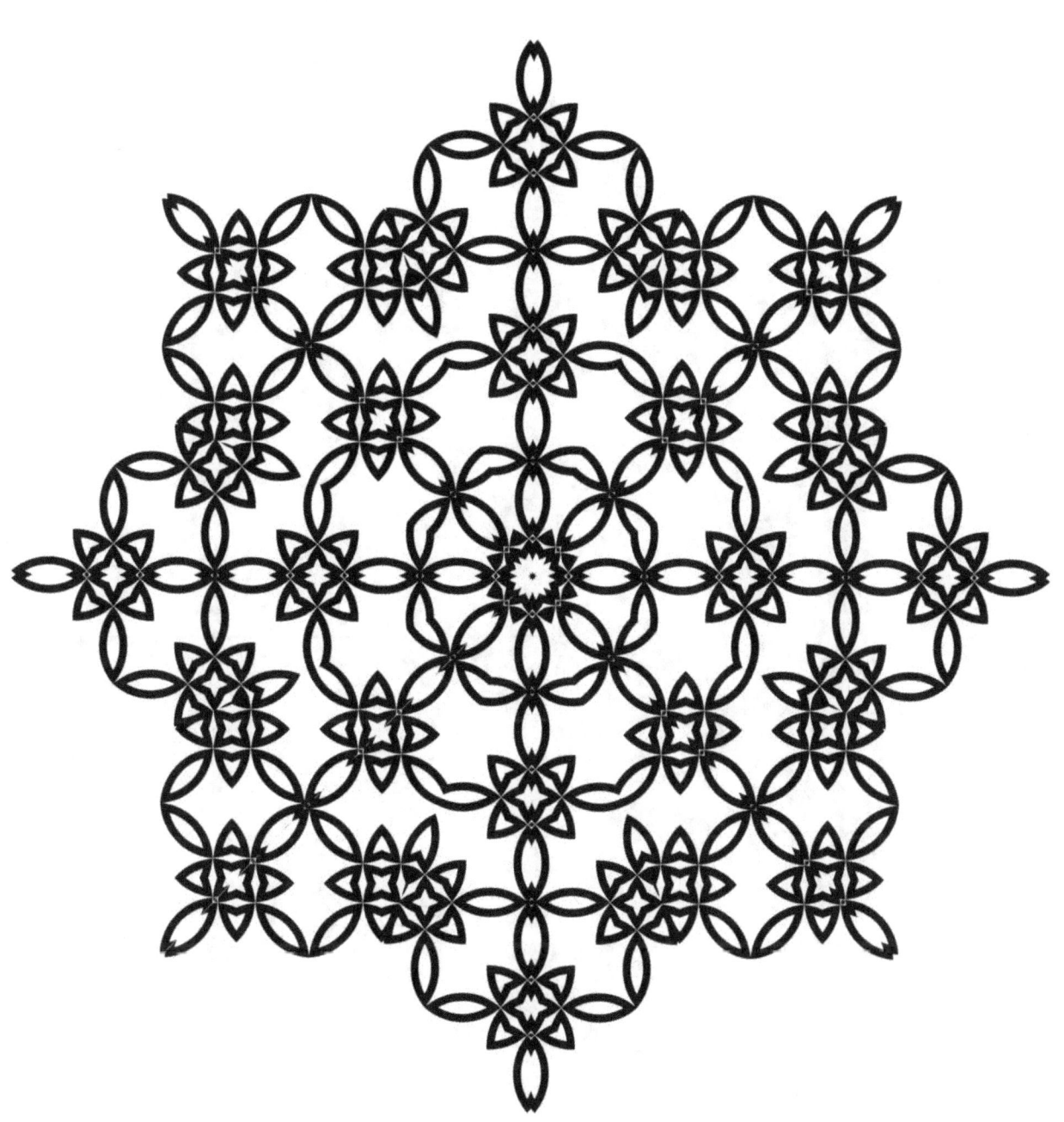

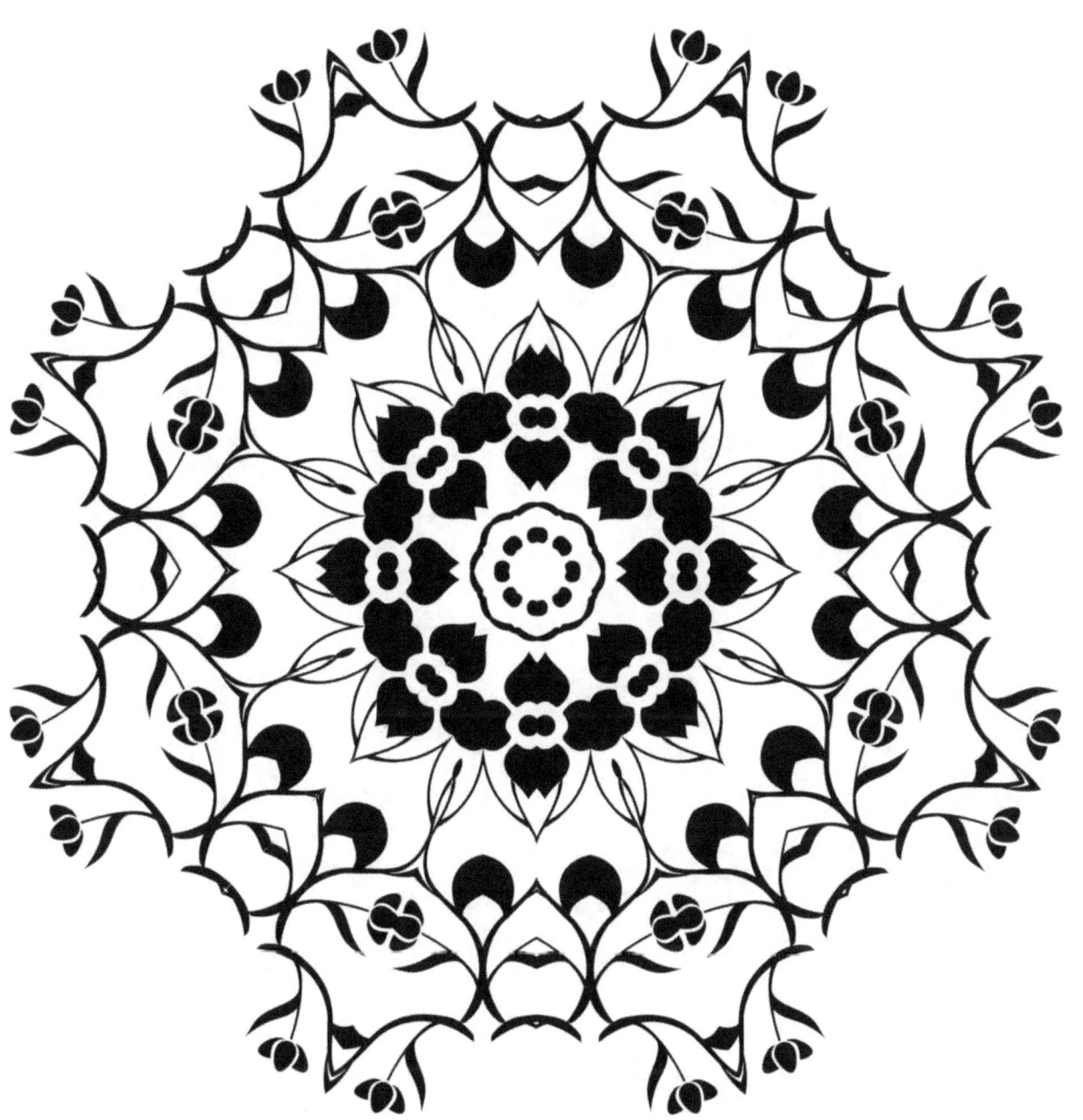

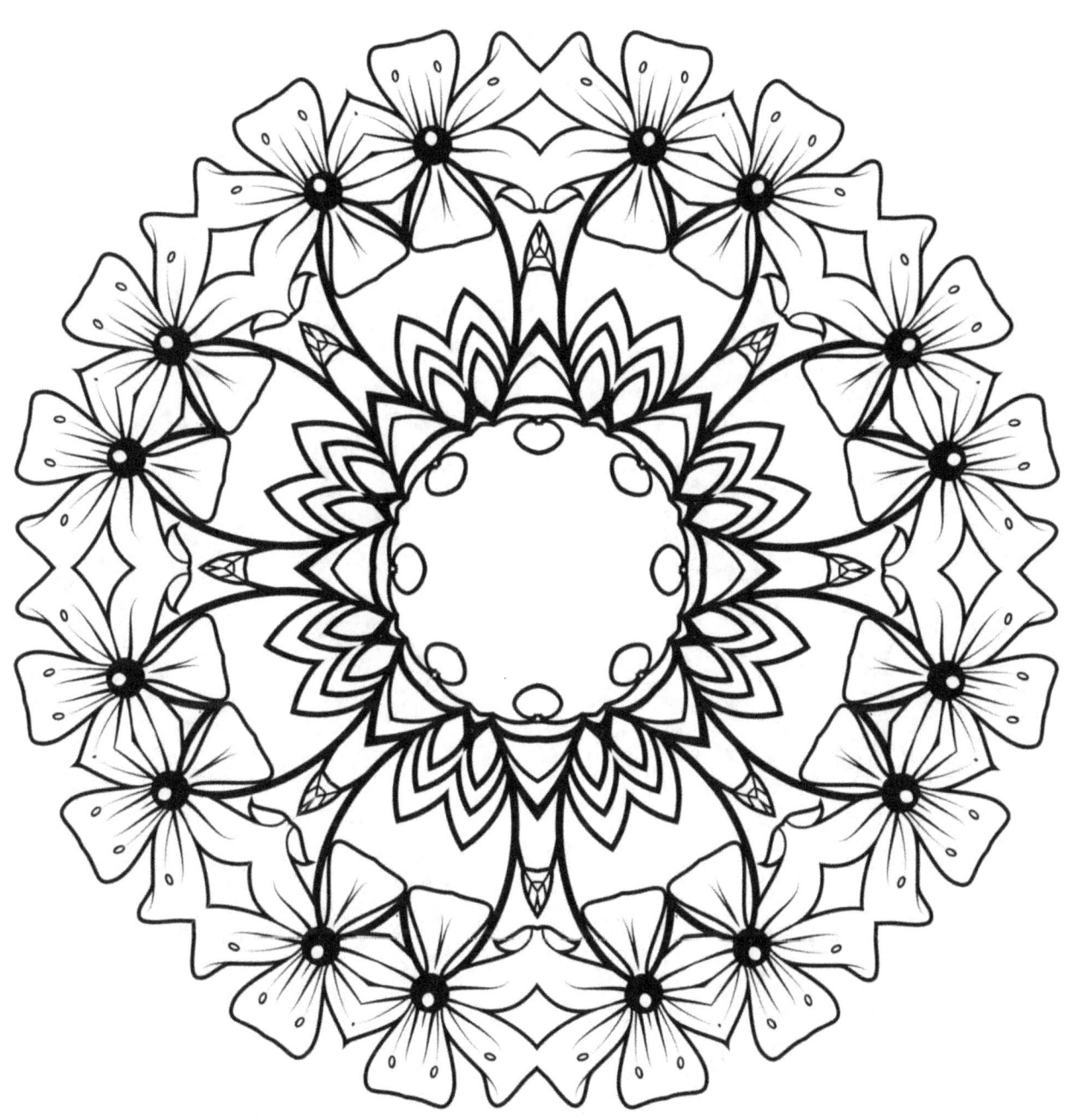

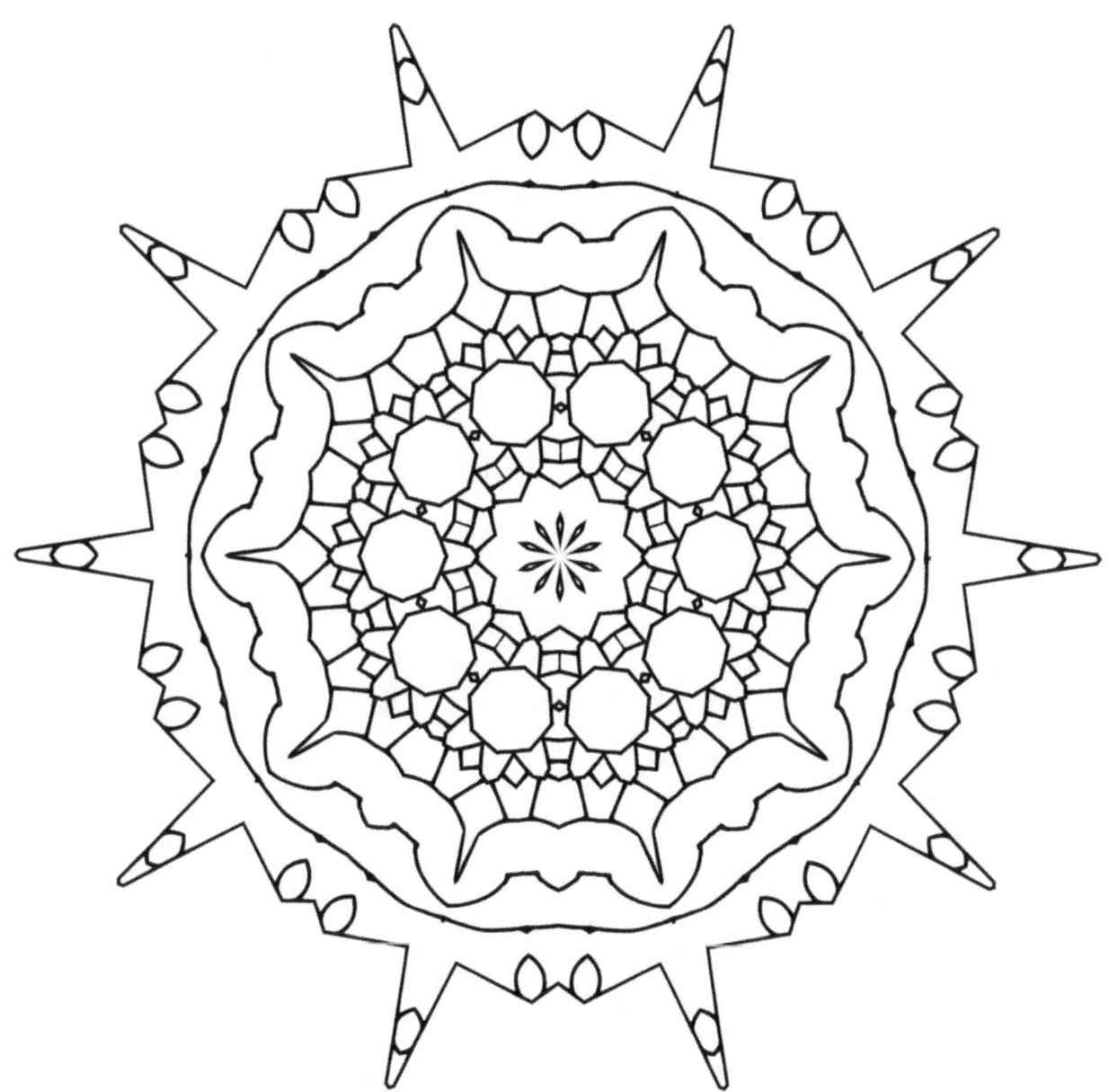

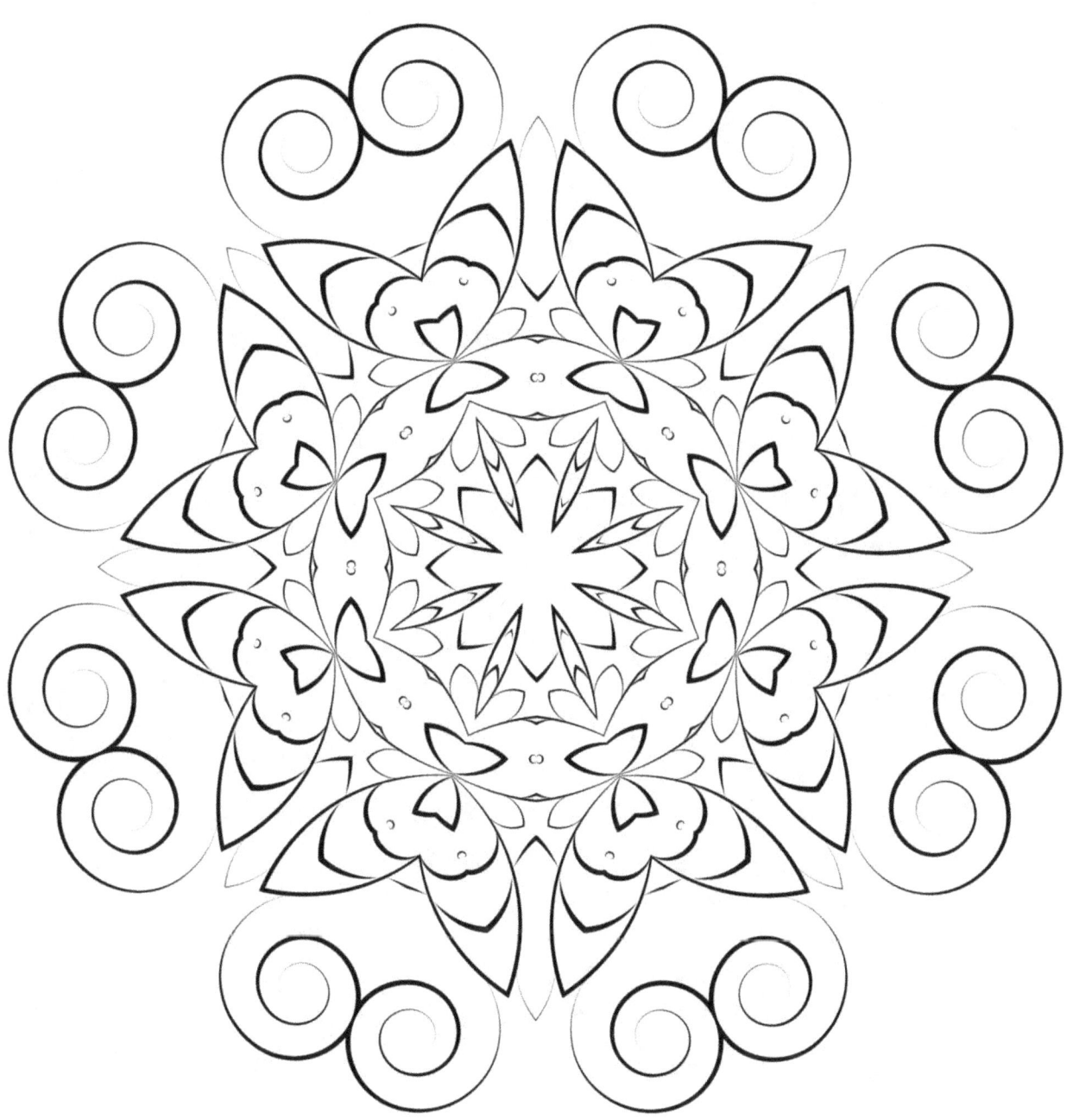

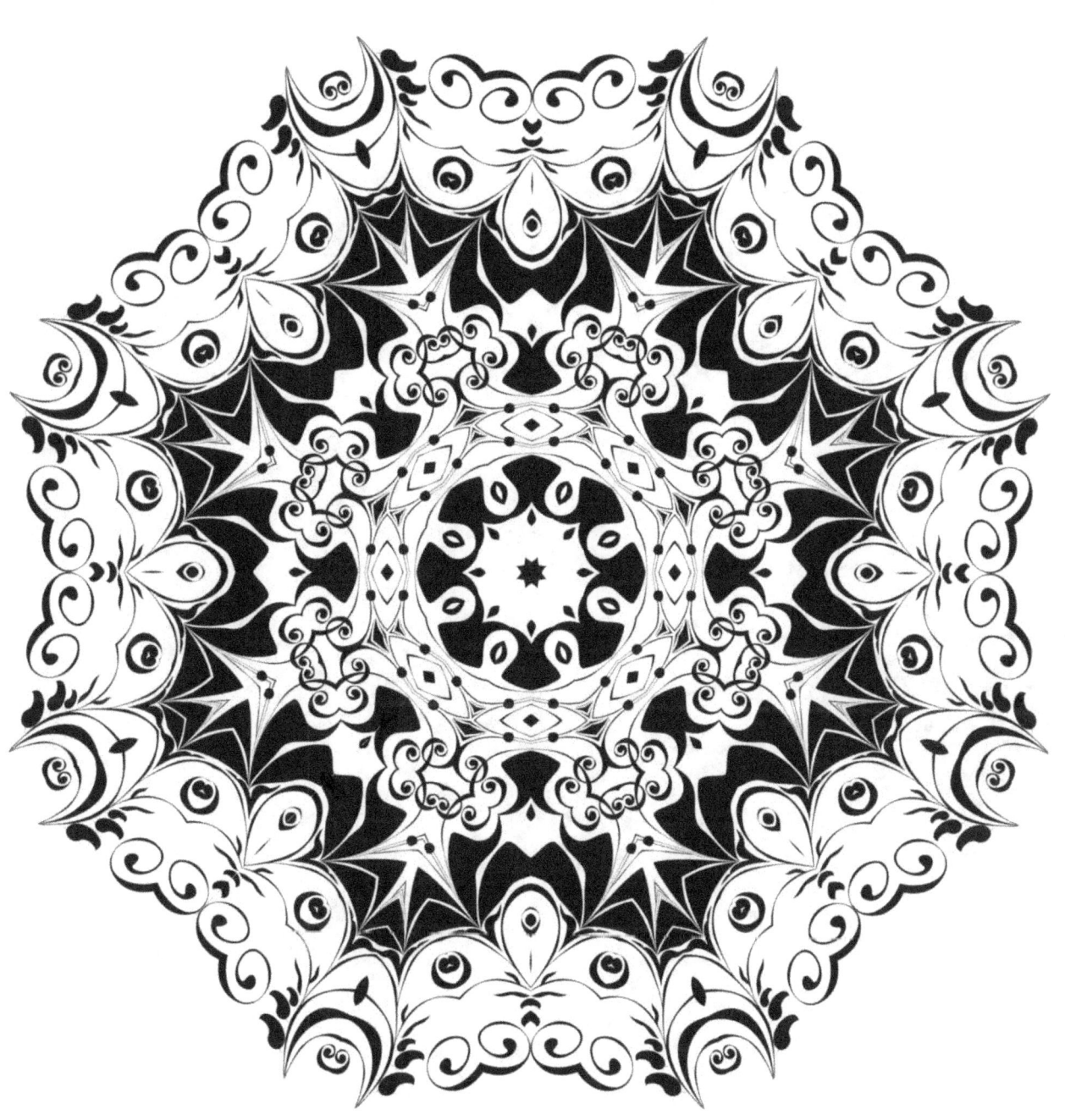

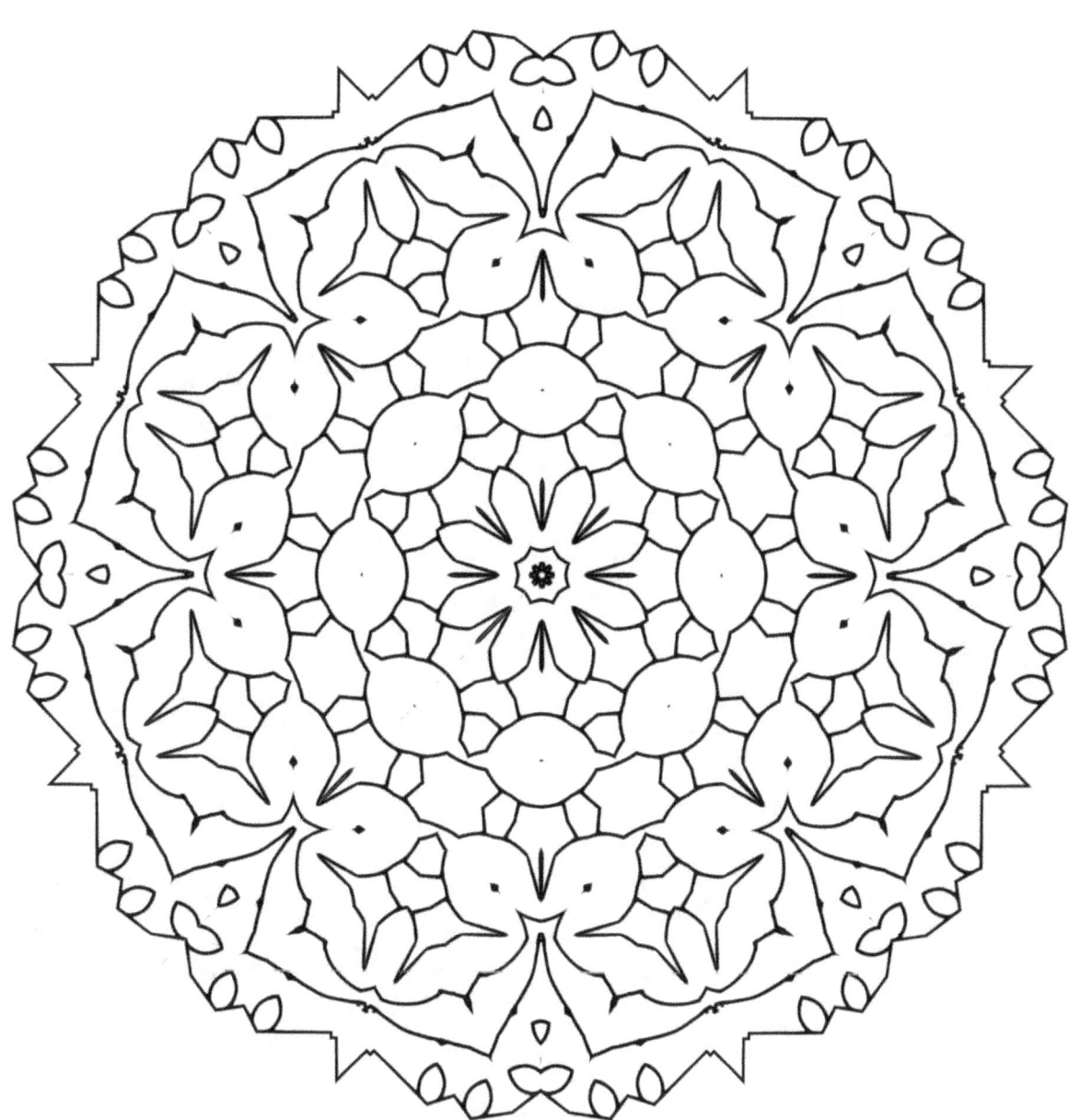

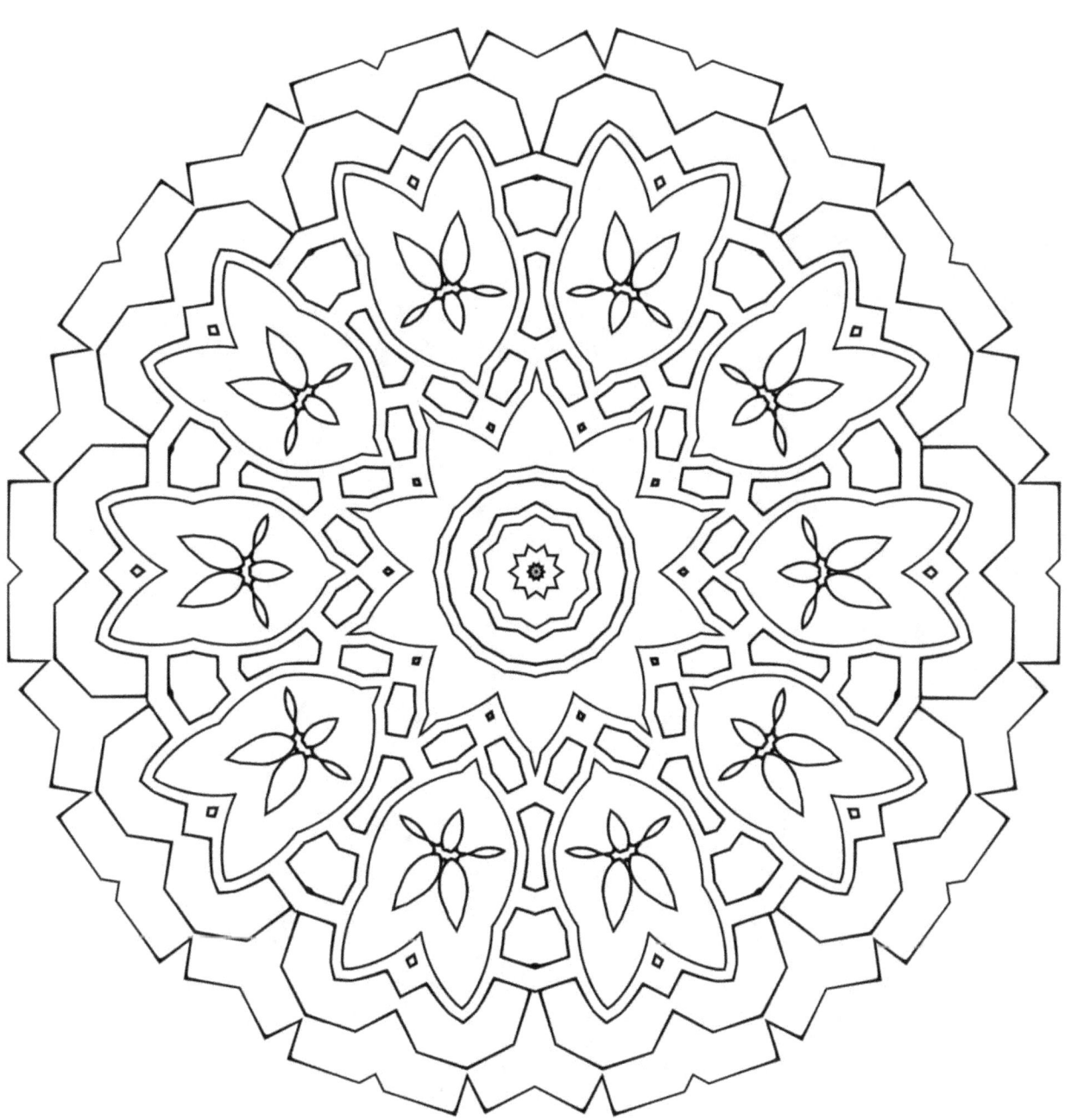

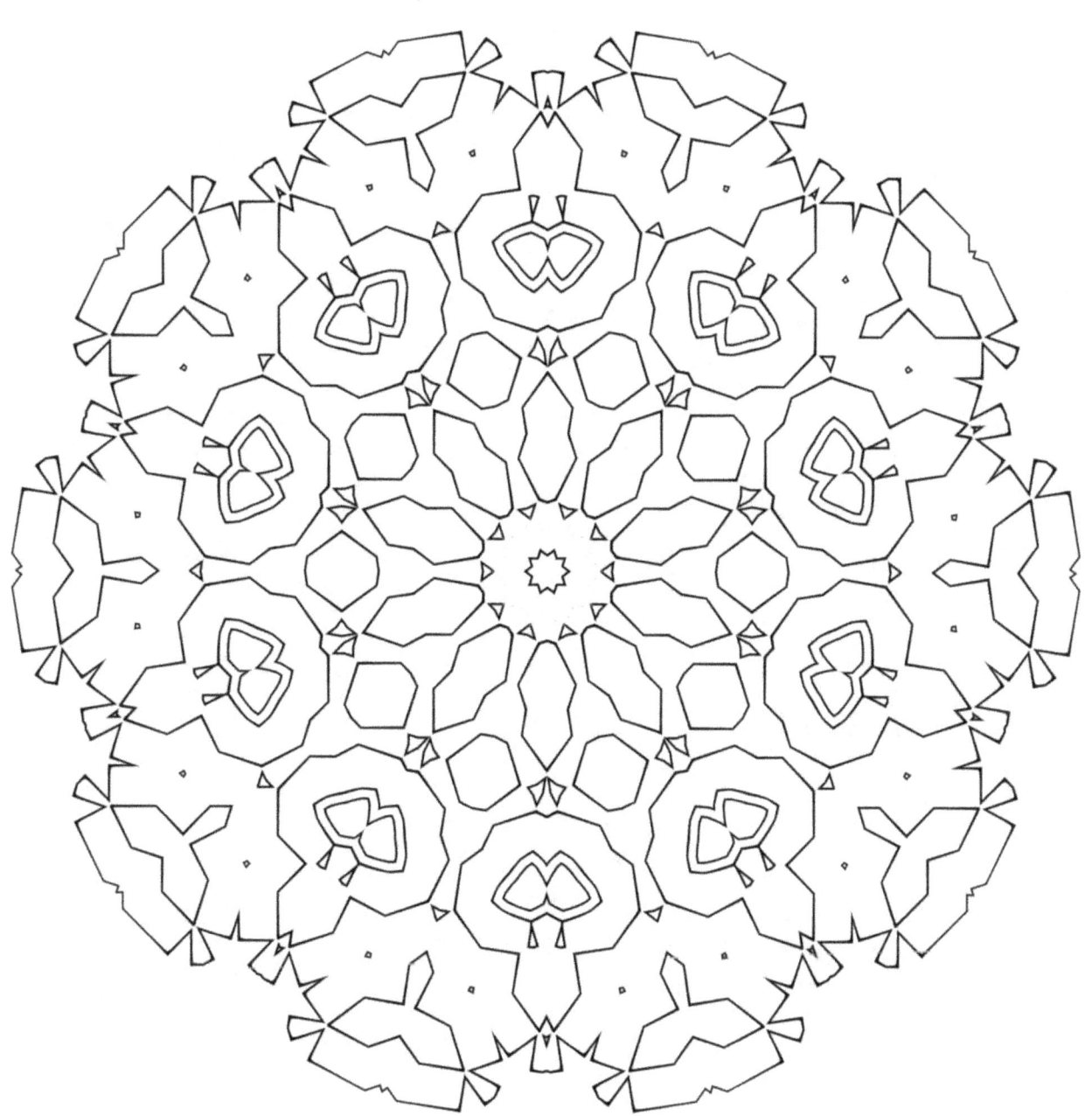

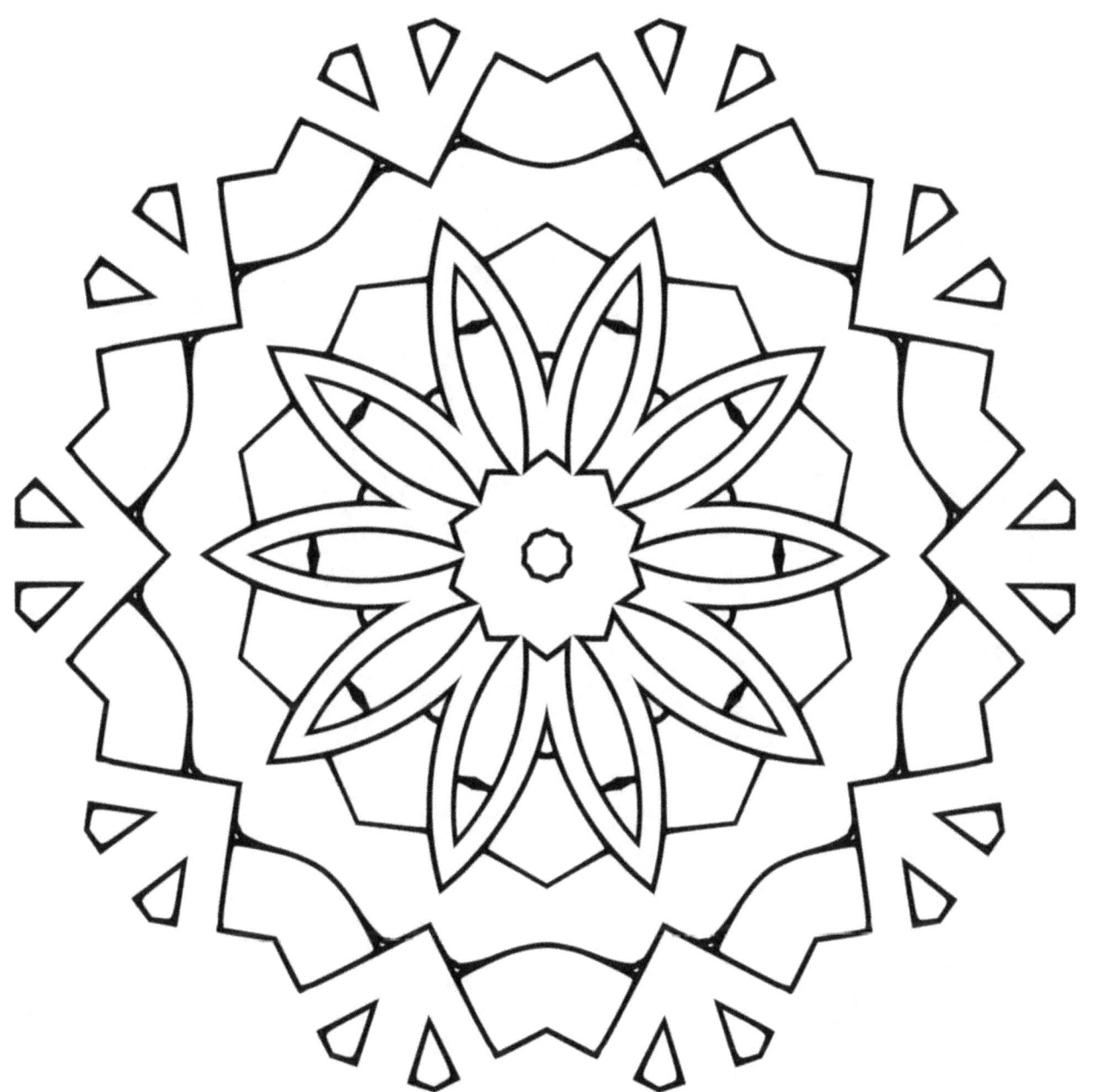

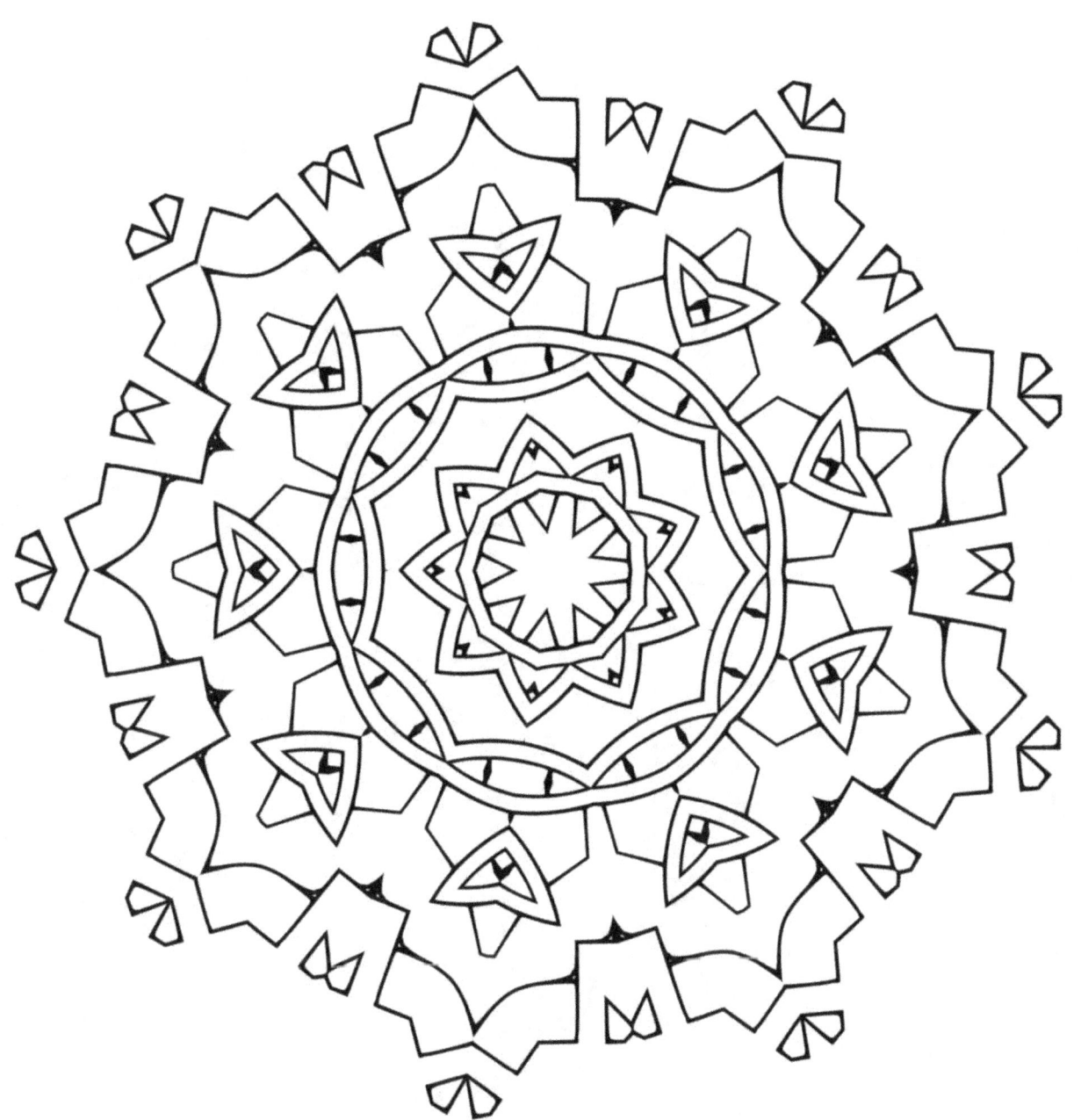

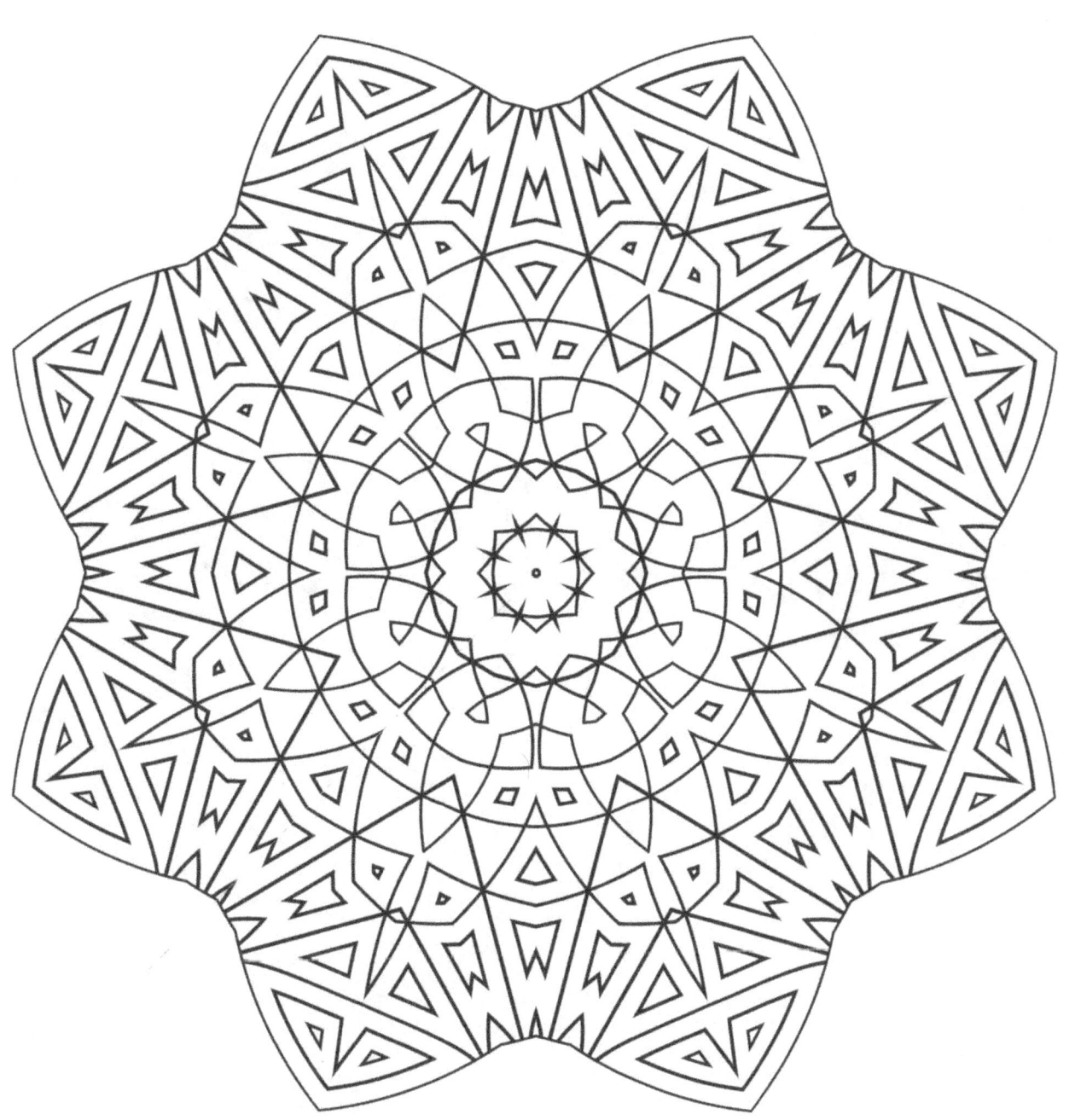

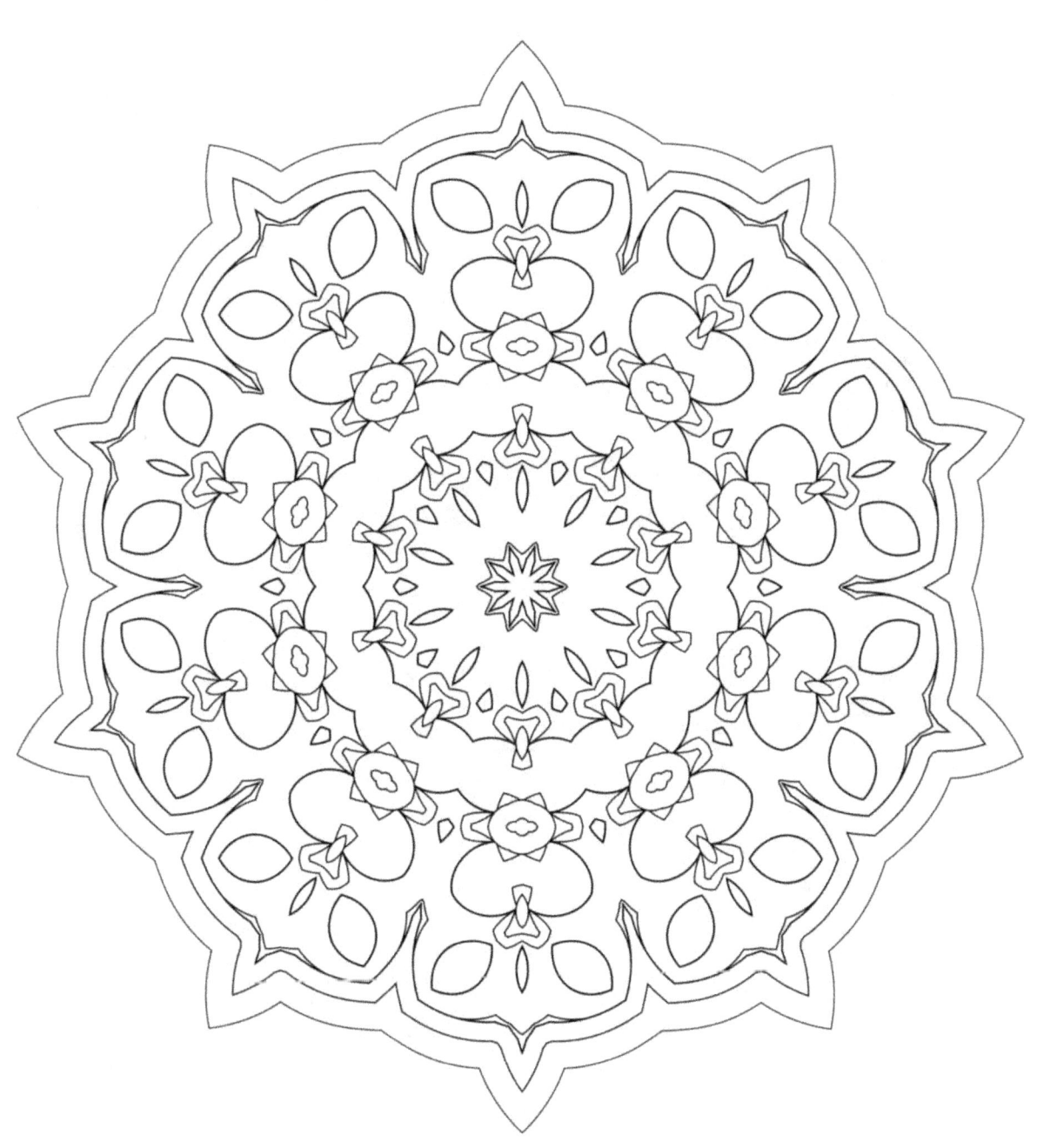

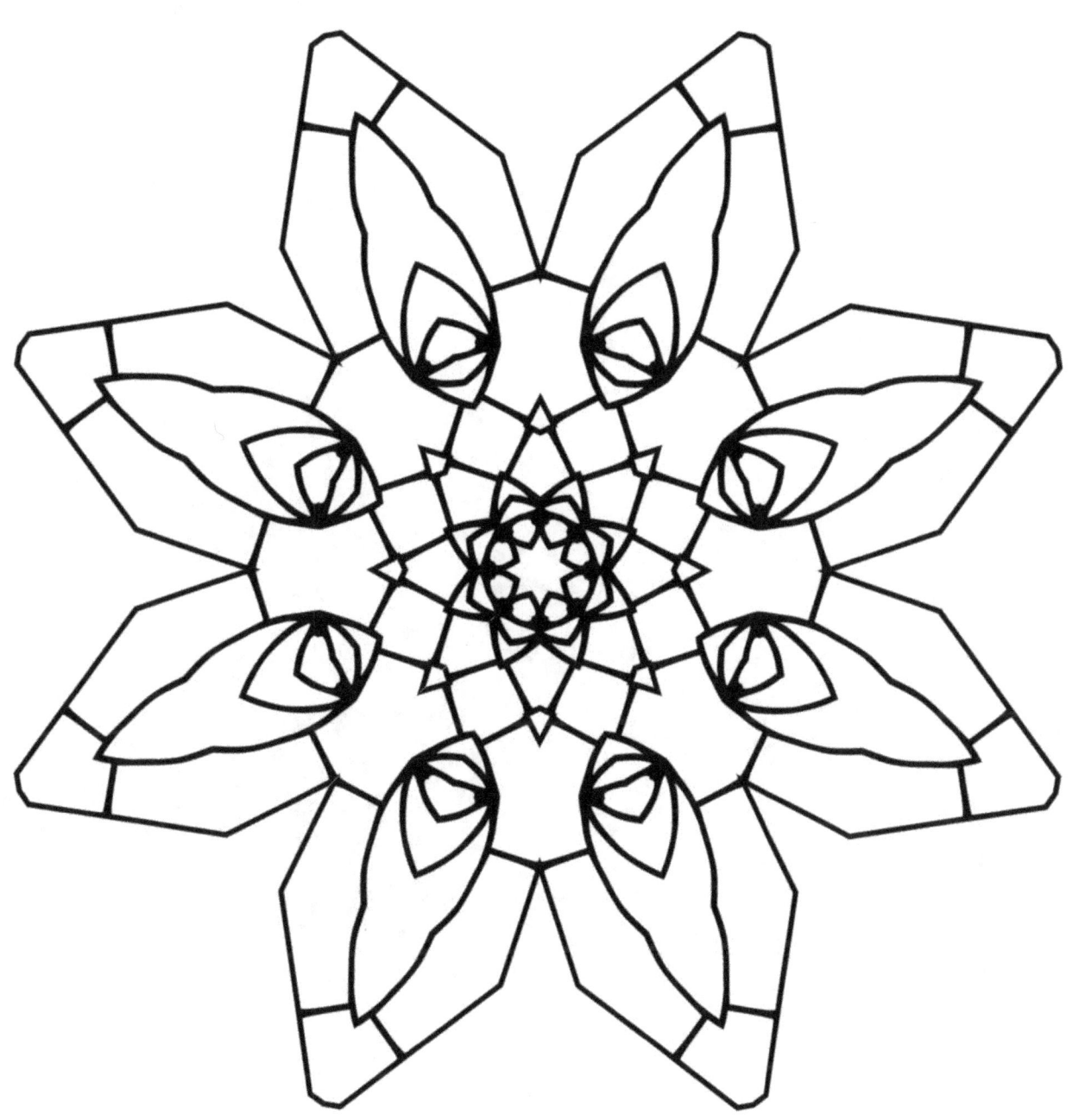

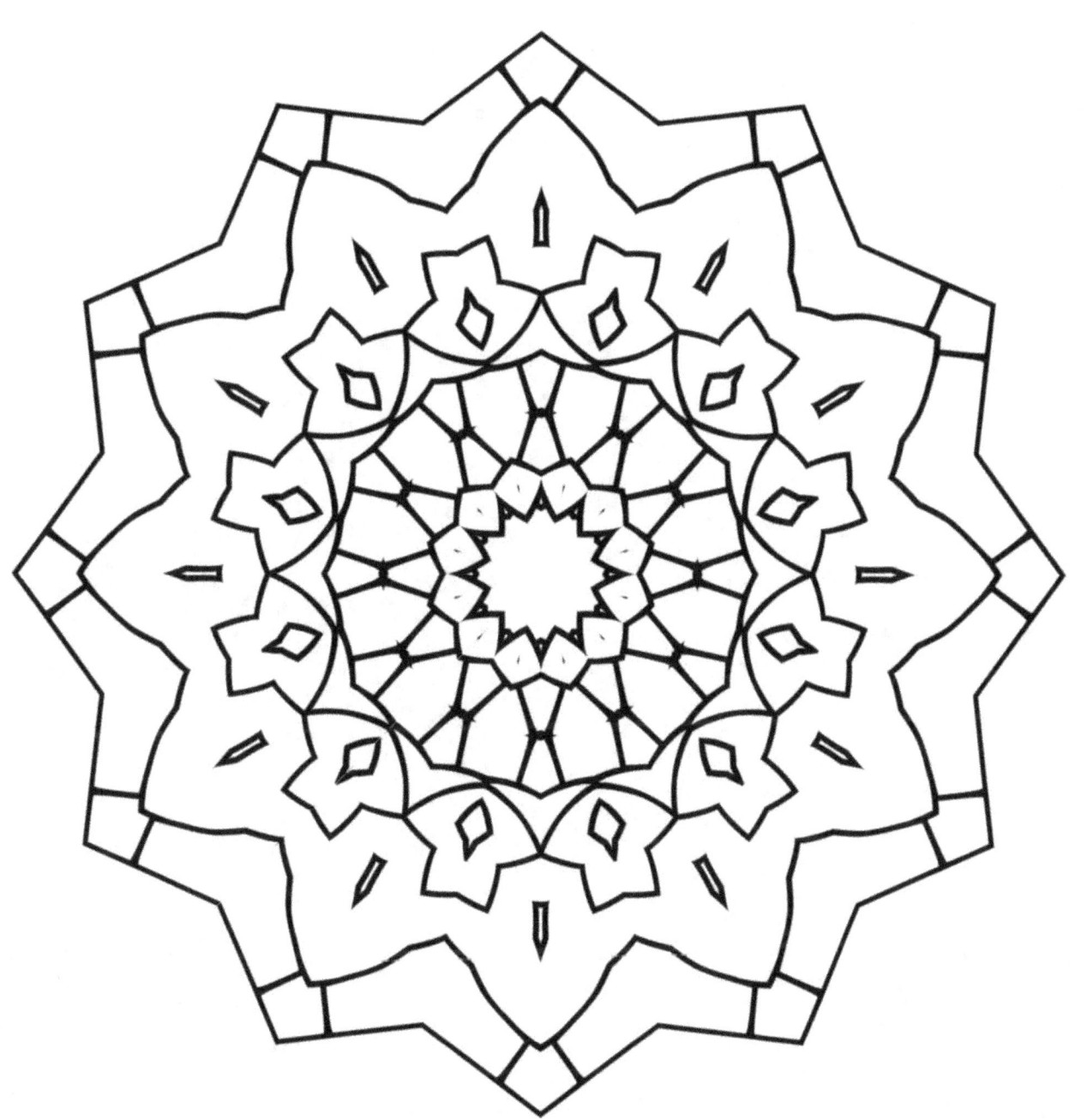

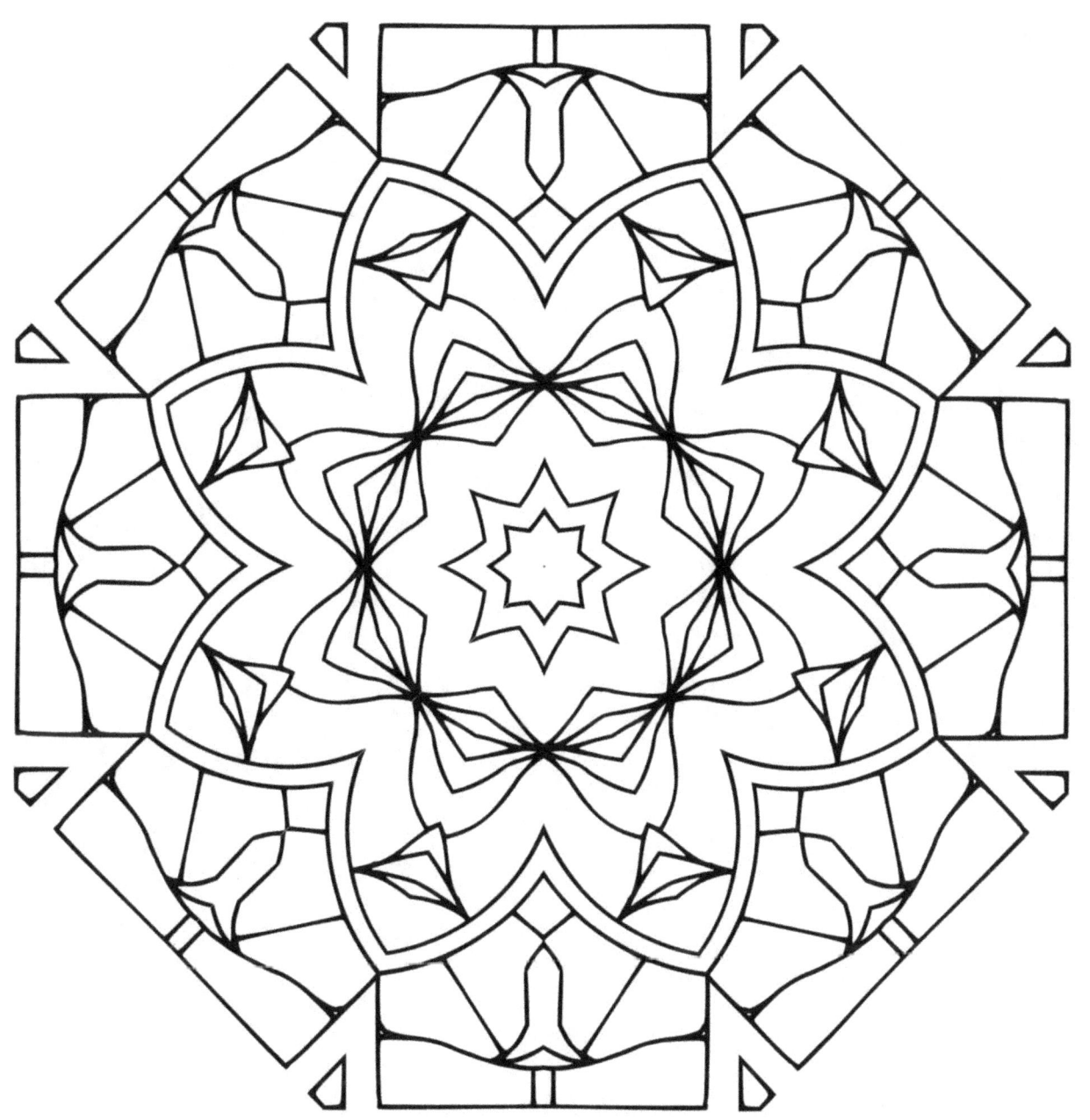

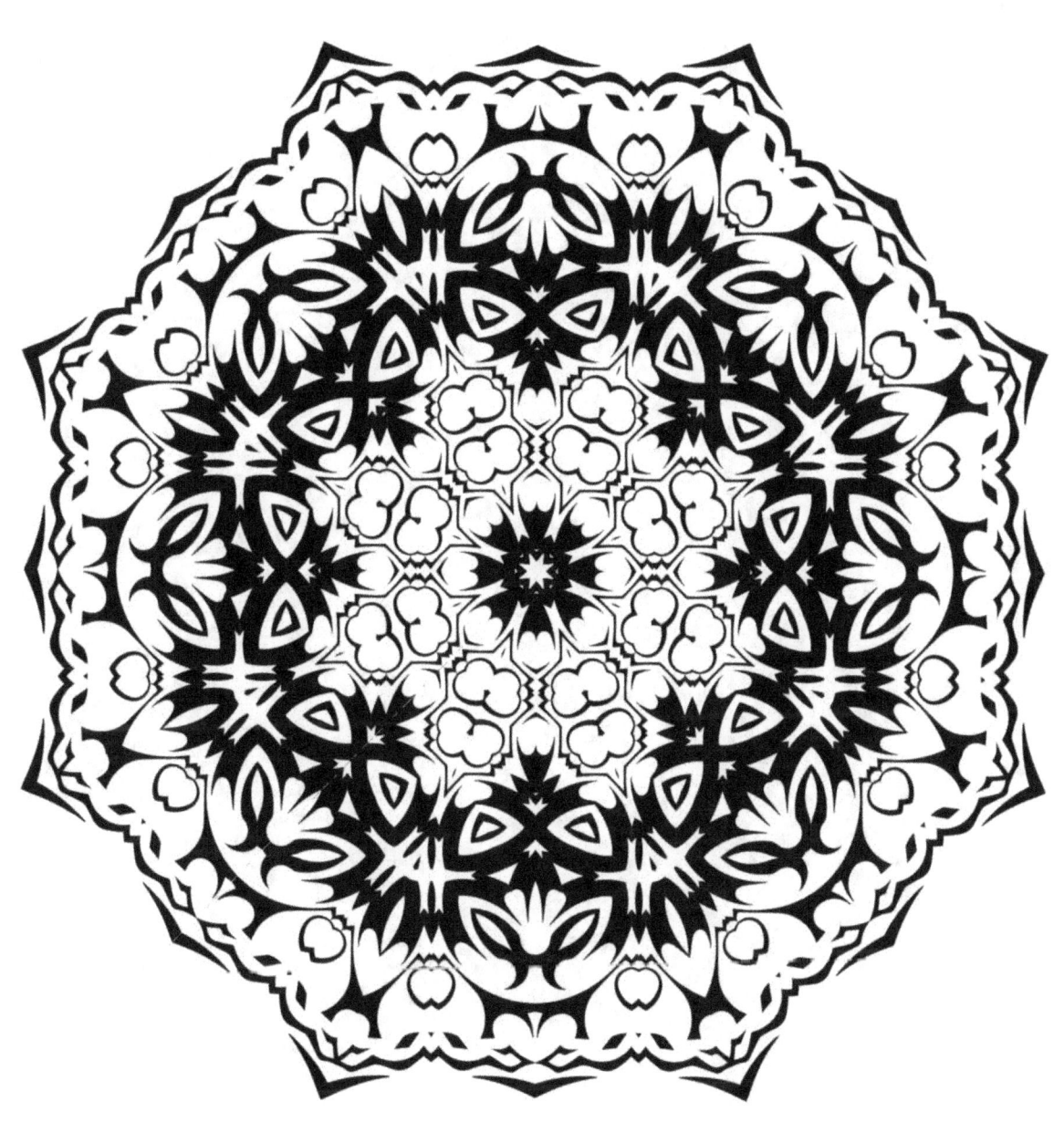

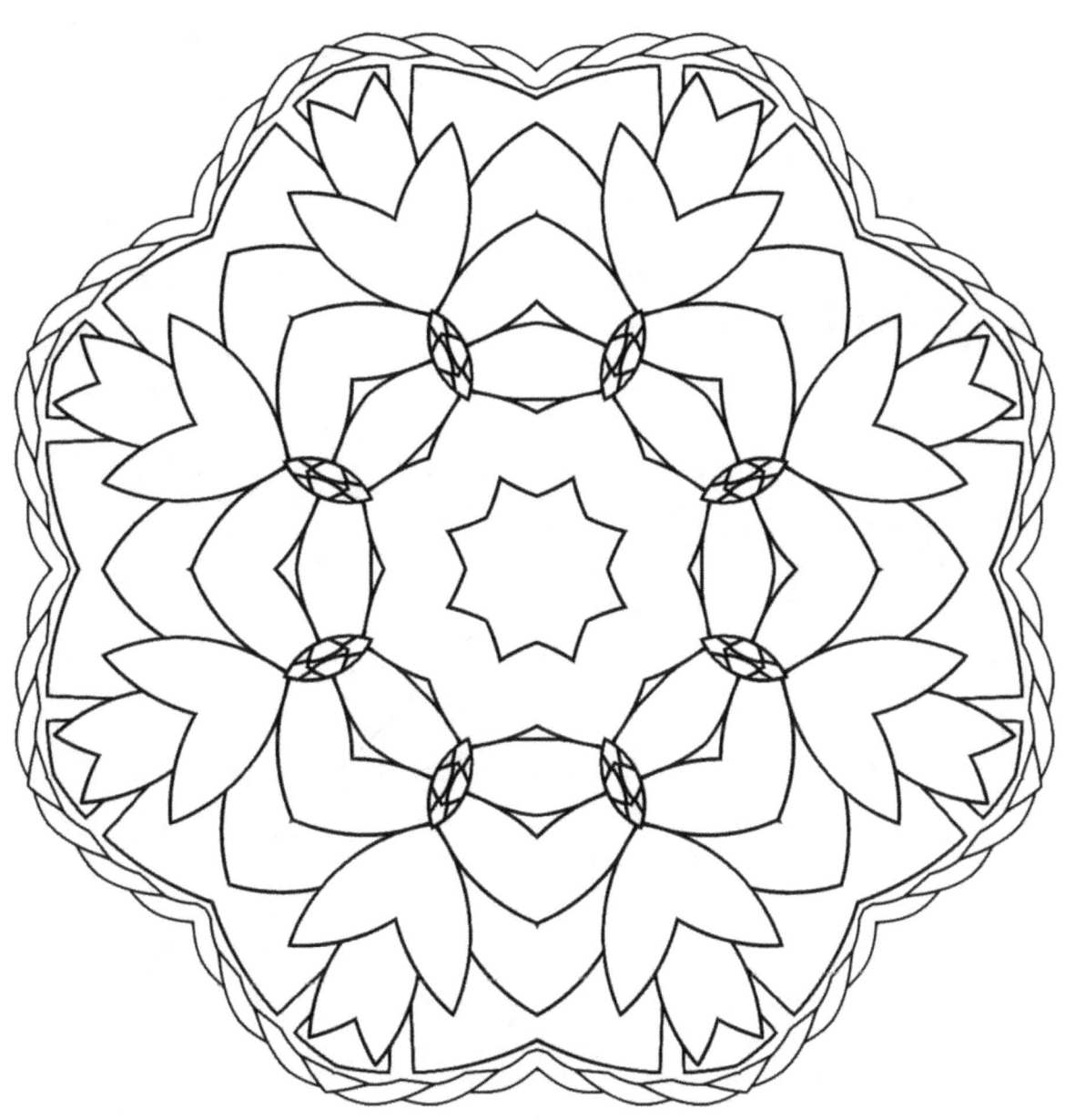

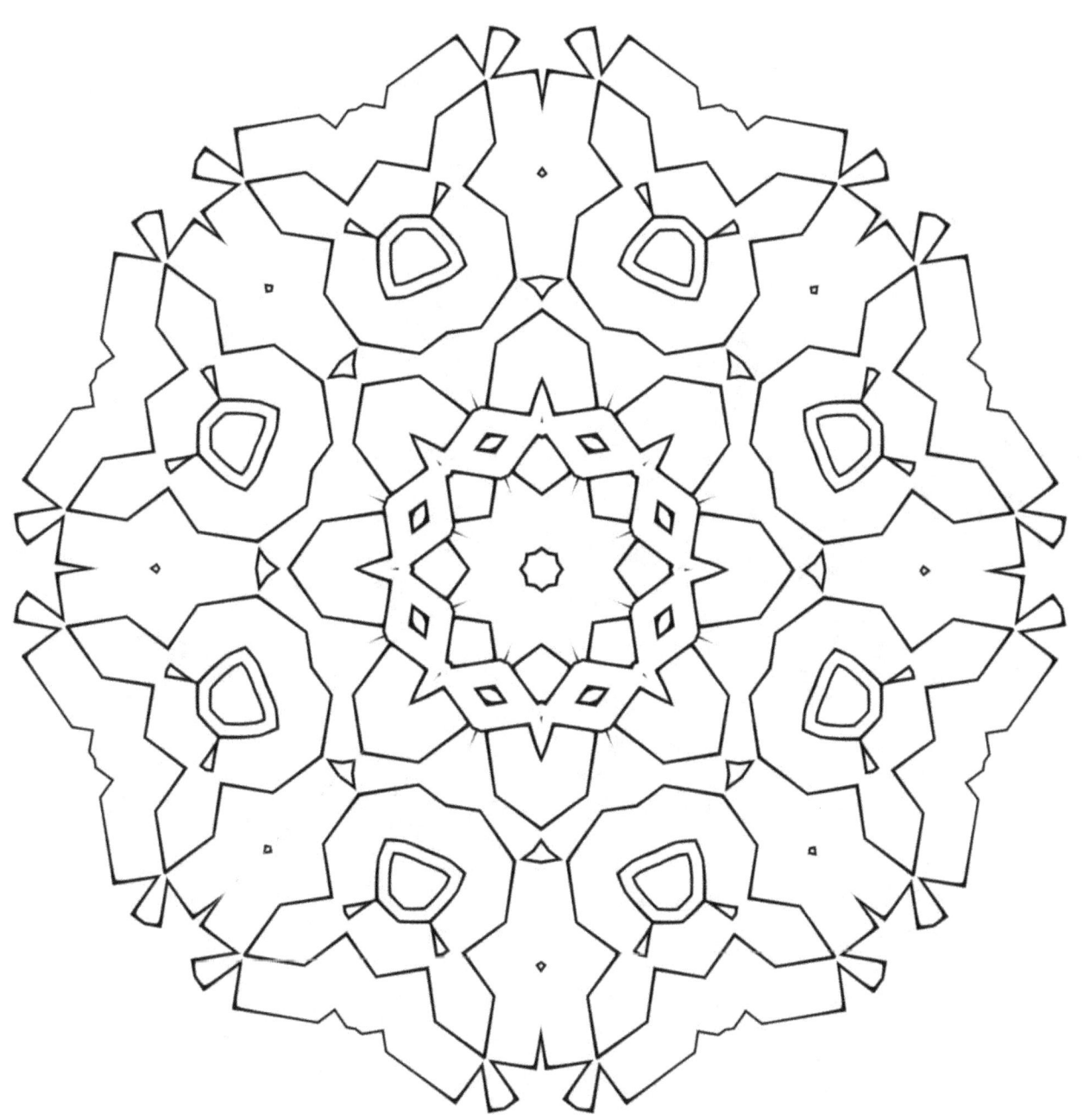

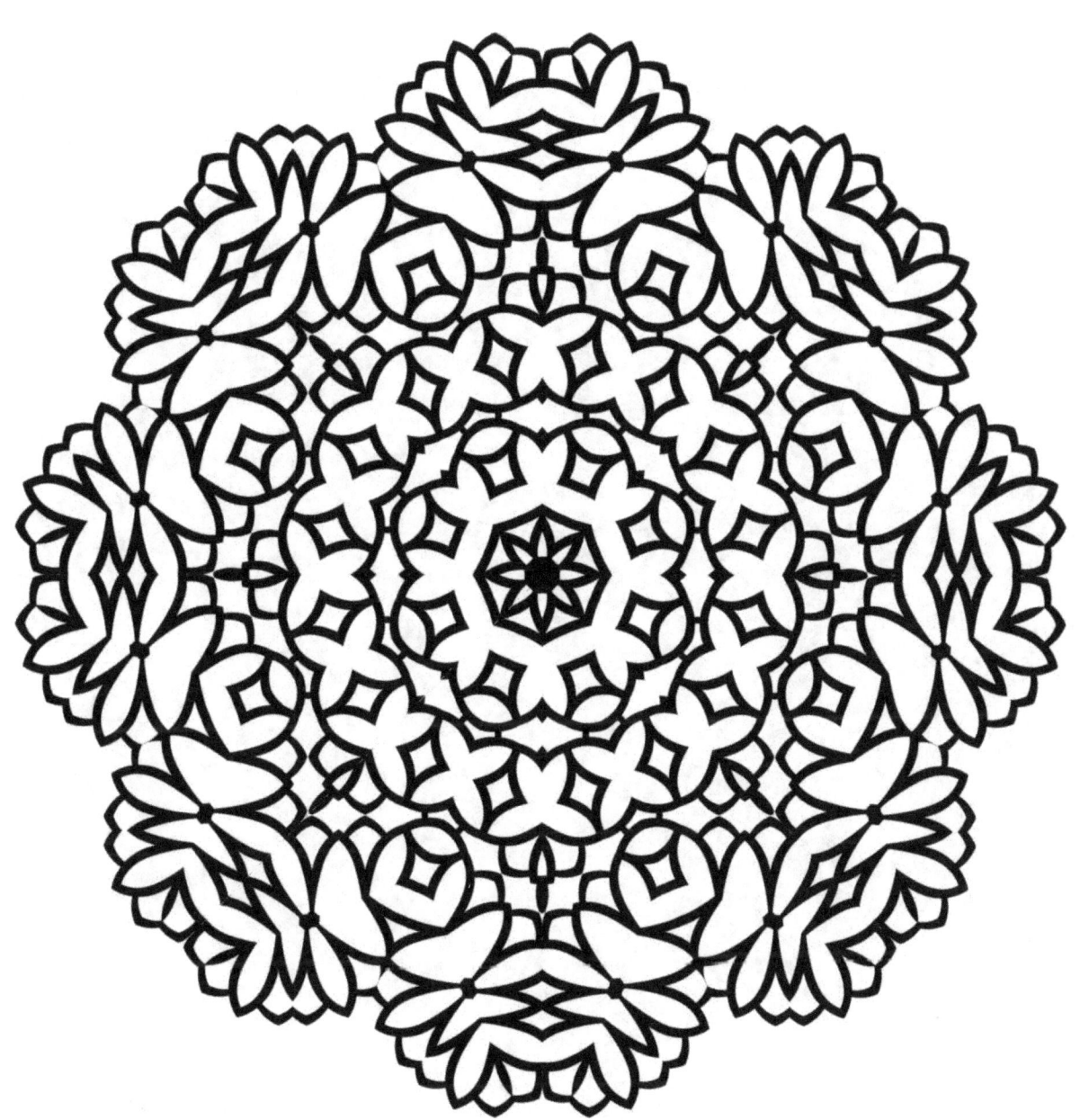

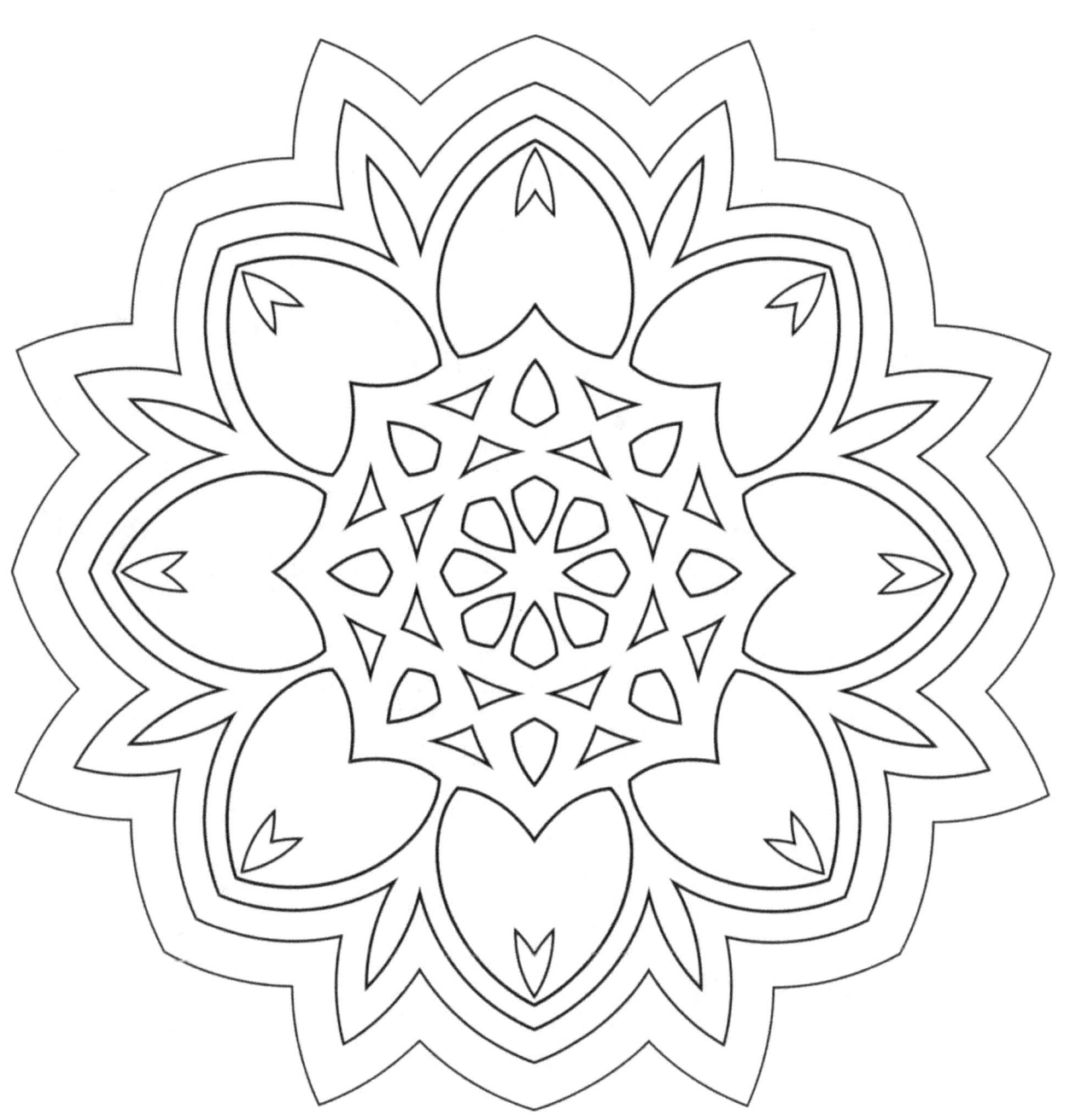

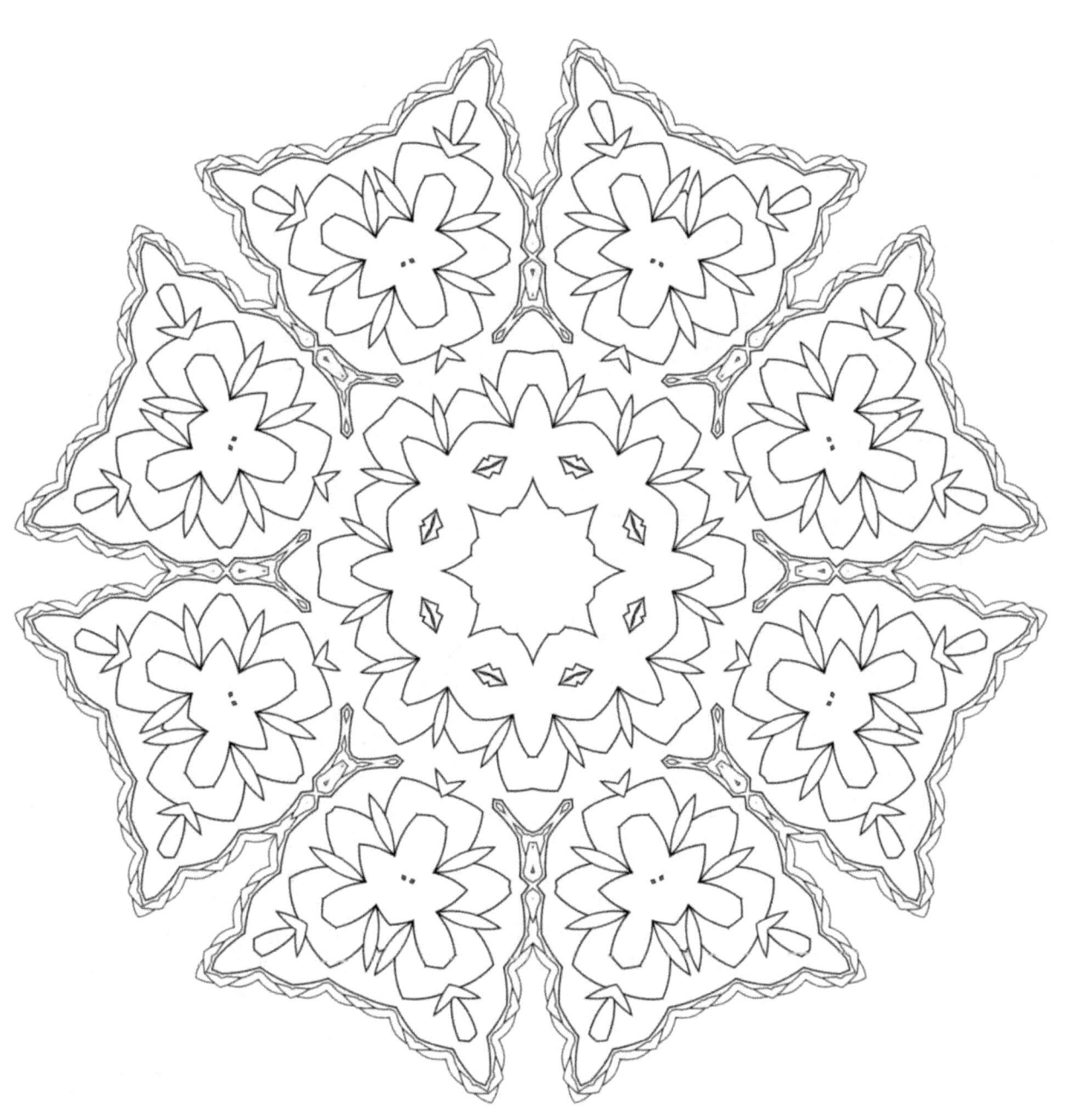

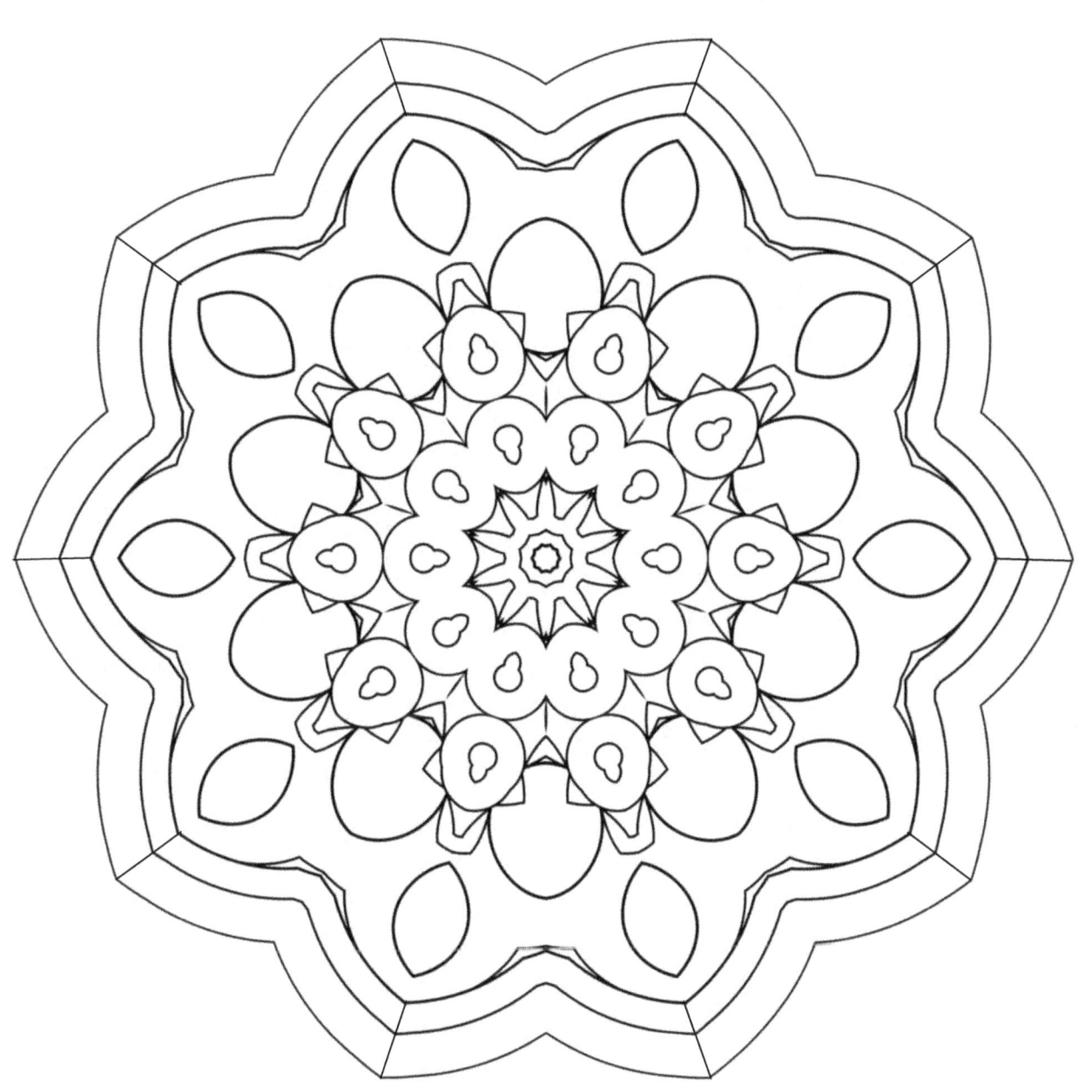

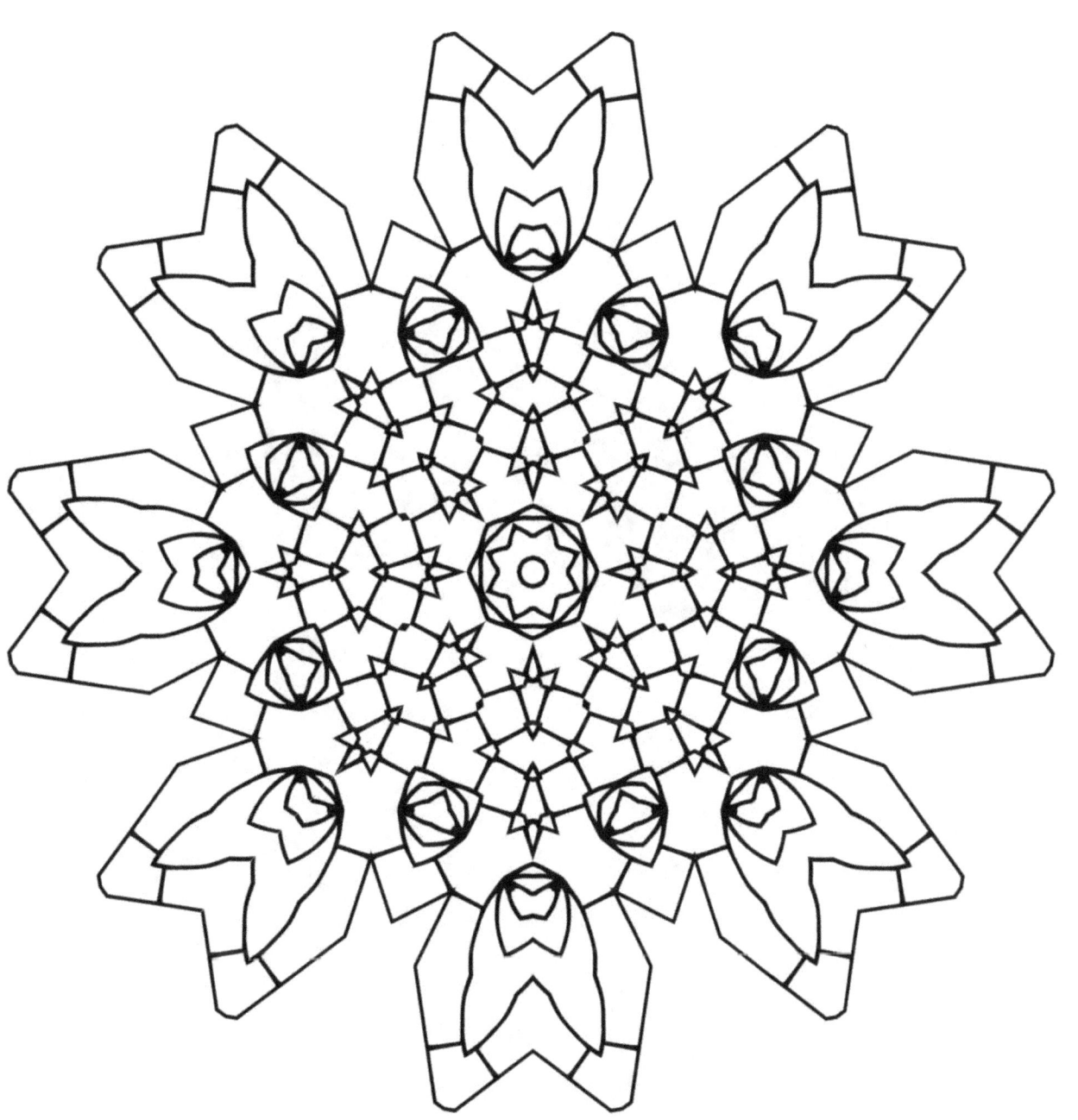

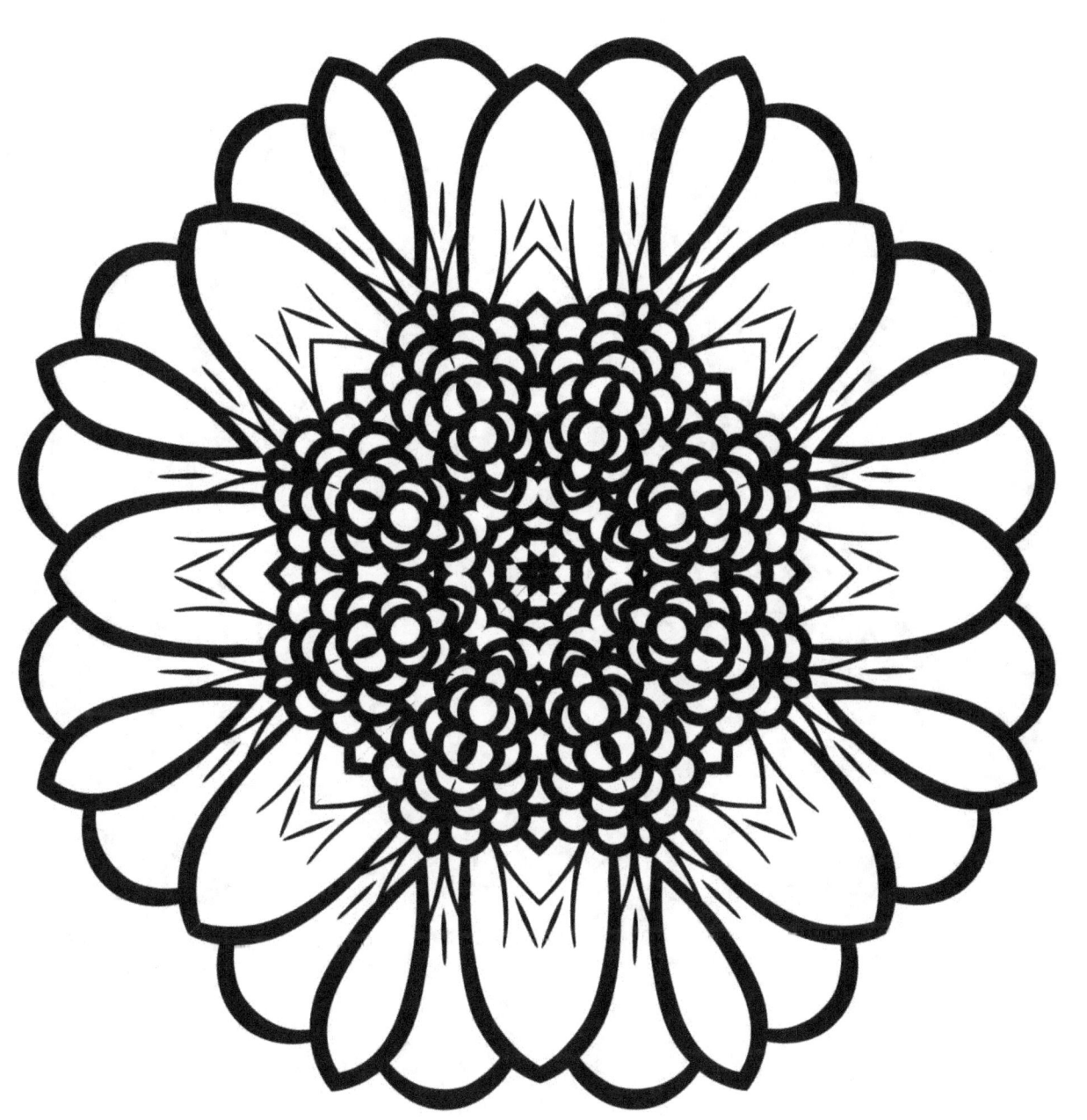

Thank you for purchasing this book!

Sign up to receive FREE weekly print-and-color patterns delivered straight to your inbox! Just type this URL into your browser: https://mirdock.leadpages.co/mariescoloring

Please check out all the books in this series:

Creative Mandala Coloring: 51 Stress-Relieving Adult Coloring Book Patterns Featuring Symmetrical & Relaxing Mandalas (Volume 1)

Creative Mandala Coloring: 51 Stress-Relieving Adult Coloring Book Patterns Featuring Symmetrical & Relaxing Mandalas (Volume 2)

Creative Mandala Coloring: 51 Stress-Relieving Adult Coloring Book Patterns Featuring Symmetrical & Relaxing Mandalas (Volume 3)

Please visit our Facebook page: https://www.facebook.com/mariescoloring

If you enjoyed this purchase, I would appreciate an honest review – *thank you!*

www.ingramcontent.com/pod-product-compliance
Lightning Source LLC
Chambersburg PA
CBHW080821180526
45168CB00006B/2532